# The Secular City Debate

# THE SECULAR
# CITY DEBATE

Edited by Daniel Callahan

THE MACMILLAN COMPANY, NEW YORK
COLLIER-MACMILLAN LTD., LONDON

Library of Congress Catalog Card Number: 66–23192

First Printing 1966

The Macmillan Company, New York
Collier-Macmillan Canada Ltd., Toronto, Ontario

PRINTED IN THE UNITED STATES OF AMERICA

### ACKNOWLEDGMENTS

I would like to express my appreciation to the following publications for permission to reprint material which first appeared in their pages:
The Anglican Theological Review for Ruel Tyson's "Urban Renewal in the Holy City." A shorter version of that article appears in this book. / Commonweal for "Beyond Bonhoeffer" by Harvey Cox; "The Secular City," by Daniel Callahan; and for the "Exchange of Views" among Andrew Greeley, Michael Novak, Daniel Callahan and Harvey Cox. / The Christian Century for Max L. Stackhouse's "Today City: Threat or Promise?" which appeared in the December 15, 1965 issue and is reprinted by permission. Copyright 1965 Christian Century Foundation. A number of small changes have been made in the version printed here. / Christianity and Crisis, July 12 and 26, 1965, for "What It Means to Be Secular," by Charles C. West; "Chalcedon in Technopolis," by Paul Lehmann; "The Social Gospel Revisited," by David Little; "Where Is the Church?" by C. Kilmer Myers; "Does The Secular City Revisit the Social Gospel?" by George D. Younger; "Secular Style and Natural Law," by Michael Novak; "Cox on His Critics," by Harvey Cox. / Christianity Today for the editorial "Supercity," which appeared on May 7, 1965. / The Presbyterian Outlook, Richmond, Virginia, for James H. Smylie's "Sons of God in the City." / Wind and Chaff for James M. Gustafson's "A Look at the Secular City." / Worldview, monthly journal published by the Council on Religion and International Affairs, for Bernard Murchland's "How Do We Speak of God Without Religion?" The version which appears here is somewhat shorter than the original. / An earlier version of George W. Peck's article "The Secular City and the Bible" appeared in the Harvard Divinity School student publication Perspectives.

# CONTENTS

v

Part Three  THE *COMMONWEAL* DEBATE

Part Four  PRESSING THE INQUIRY FURTHER

Part Five  HARVEY COX RESPONDS

# Introduction

Every book has an uncertain future, and this is all the more true at that expectant moment, just prior to publication, when publisher and author begin to wonder what the public will make of it. I divulge no secrets when I say that the reception given *The Secular City* astounded both The Macmillan Company and Harvey Cox. After all, most of the themes discussed by Cox—secularization, urbanization, anonymity, theological language, and so on—have been discussed by almost everyone in the past decade. There was no special reason to expect that still another book on these matters would create any kind of stir. Nor was the author particularly well known to the general public. Nonetheless, within a short time *The Secular City* had gone into multiple printings. "Hands down," *Christian Century* could say, "Protestantism's most discussed book [in 1965] was Harvey Cox's affirmative evaluation of the modern megalopolis, *The Secular City.*" And I can attest from my own experience as an editor of a Catholic periodical that Cox's book aroused unusual interest in the Roman Catholic community.

Superficially at least, it is not hard to guess at some of the reasons. Within Protestantism, the influence of Dietrich Bonhoeffer was beginning to be felt outside of academic circles, and, in part, Cox's book represents one way of coming to grips with Bonhoeffer's themes of a "world come of age" and a "religionless Christianity." Then again, it would probably be accurate to say that existentialism has lost some of its bloom in theology; undoubtedly, Cox's strictures against existentialist modes of thought found some public resonances. The shifts and developments in the civil-rights movement suggest still another reason. The year 1965 saw a waning of the earlier emphasis on legal rights for Southern Negroes (partially because of the successful passage of the Civil Rights Acts of 1964 and 1965) and an intensified effort to

1

confront the massive difficulties of Northern urban Negroes.
This concern inevitably focused attention on the myriad
complexities of modern urban life. Could the cities be saved?
What should be the quality of their life? Does urbanization
necessarily spell an end to rich human relationships, human
freedom, and human development? These have become ines-
capable questions, and the vast output on Protestant writings
on urbanization, the number of urban missions and experimental churches attest to their centrality in Protestant
thought.

From the Roman Catholic side, 1965 saw the end of the
Second Vatican Council. More and more, as the Council
moved through its four tempestuous sessions, it was seen that
the "Church in the modern world" was perhaps the most
important issue of all. The passage of the decree on that
subject, at the end of the fourth session, was a signal and an
expression of Roman Catholicism's sudden awakening to the
world about it. Cox's book appeared in the midst of the
debate which preceded the passage of the decree; it could
hardly have been more timely. That it happened to be written
by a Protestant was almost irrelevant. Light was (and is)
needed, and the growing success of ecumenical discussion
helped to lessen any Catholic worries about turning to a
Protestant for illumination. There were other changes as well.
If few Roman Catholics had heard of Bonhoeffer, they had
begun to hear of "secularization" as a concept and reality
distinguishable from "secularism" (they had heard of the latter *ad nauseam*). And the city was beginning to be seen in far
more constructive ways than it had in the past. Again, it is
likely that Cox's characterization of John F. Kennedy as an
example of the Christian pragmatic man helped to pinpoint
the late President's attraction for many Catholics trying to
develop a new style of Christian life.

But these are speculations only, and they completely ignore
the intrinsic merits of *The Secular City*.

The purpose of the present book is modest. It aims neither
to celebrate Cox's book nor to provide a forum for those
critical of the book. Instead, it is simply a collection of published reactions to the book, plus some essays written ex-
pressly for this book. As such, it is meant for those who

might find it useful as a companion volume to Cox's work, bringing together under one cover the responses of a diverse group of readers. I was encouraged in this project by the success and utility of David L. Edwards' book *The Honest to God Debate*. I hope he will forgive me for so brazenly imitating his idea and his title.

This book is divided into five parts. The first section comprises a number of book reviews and articles which appeared in different periodicals. By and large, this material appears as it was originally published, although in a few cases the authors kindly consented to rework their original comments for the sake of brevity. In some cases, I have edited passages which simply summarized the contents of *The Secular City*. The second section consists of the essays and rejoinders which appeared in *Christianity and Crisis*. This section also includes Professor Cox's reply to these essays (which also appeared in *Christianity and Crisis*). The third section consists of an exchange published in *Commonweal*. The fourth section is made up of four essays written at my request for this book.

The final section is by Harvey Cox. It was his good fortune that *The Secular City* provoked enough interest to suggest the value of a companion volume of comments. At the same time, it must be said that the praise which appears herein is more than balanced by pointed criticism. I will have to confess, in fact, that I chose not to include a number of published reviews because they seemed to me too uncritically enthusiastic about the book. In any case, it seems fitting to let Professor Cox have the last word here.

Though somewhat off the specific topic of this collection, I have also included, in an appendix, an article on Bonhoeffer which Cox published in *Commonweal*.

It remains only for me to thank those who made this book possible: the various publishers who gave permission for the reprinting of the articles and reviews; those authors who, working with a tight deadline, wrote especially for this book; and Harvey Cox, for consenting to write the final essay. Without their assistance this book would not have been possible.

Daniel Callahan

# PART ONE

# WHAT THE REVIEWERS SAID

# CHAPTER 1

# Sons of God in the City

*James H. Smylie*

*The Secular City*, conveniently packaged in paperback and flashingly written, will have a wide market. Cox has already been called daring by *Time* and feted in a whole issue of *Christianity and Crisis*. He is "in," and we may expect a widespread discussion of secularization *à la* the associate professor of church and society in the Harvard Divinity School.

Handwringing by the Christian over secularization is unbecoming and unnecessary, according to the author. The secular city is a manifestation of Christian faith and life, not antagonistic to it nor to be deplored and despised. It is connected with the collapse of traditional religion and the rise of urban civilization. Christians should celebrate its liberties and accept its discipline. The secular city is postmythical and postmetaphysical and therefore a threat only to tribalists and townsmen who attempt to live in contemporary urban society on the basis of presuppositions no longer viable.

Urbanization is not simply a quantitative term. It is the sign of secularization; it is man's task and man's responsibility. Cox celebrates the shape, style, and even the organization of the city. Its shape involves anonymity, attacked by some who misunderstand it as dehumanizing, but interpreted by Cox as protecting humanity from the oppressive determination of the law. Its shape also involves mobility, attacked by the reactionary who clings to permanence, but interpreted by Cox as deliverance from immobile gods of place which kill life. The style of the city involves the functional-pragmatic approach to truth and its unity, summarized in the question "Will it work?" and embodied in John F. Kennedy. Its style includes profanity, "having to do with this world" outside the temple and embodied in the French writer Albert Camus.

Bureaucratic organization in the city, discussed by Cox in his treatment of work and play, is not a cause for continual self-laceration. This organization, operating at its best, involves needed flexibility, orientation toward the future, limitation of the city's claims, and above all secularization. Life does not depend upon gods of myth or metaphysics, but upon personal decision and responsible control and exercise of power.

How are Christians responsible for this secularization? According to theologian-sociologist Cox, Christians have worshiped and witnessed to the God of the Bible, who is "at once different *from* man, unconditionally *for* man, and entirely *unavailable* for coercion and manipulation *by* man." Cox begins with the Old Testament categories. The category of Creation, involves the *disenchantment* of nature; the Exodus, the *desacralization* of politics; the Sinai Covenant, which forbade the worship of idols, the *deconsecration* of values. The *Deus Absconditus* of the Bible is known best in political terms, disclosing himself in doing for man. This activity is best manifested in the "life of Jesus of Nazareth," who is the embodiment of the Kingdom and who remains "the fullest possible disclosure of the partnership of God and man in history." Cox suggests that the Kingdom is "in process of realizing itself," as he interprets eschatology in terms of what occurs between Easter and the Last Day. Christians have been God's people. Today, they should be His avant-garde, always remembering that in this life catastrophe and catharsis come again and again. Christian ministry continues the ministry of Jesus, as it fulfills a threefold responsibility of *Kerygma* (proclamation), *diakonia* (reconciliation, healing, and other forms of service), and *koinonia* (a demonstration of the character of the new society). Christian ministry is maturely to frame with the neighbor "a common life suitable to the secular city" and to prevent secularization from becoming secular*ism,* an ideology, a closed world view which functions like religion in an attempt to manipulate God.

Concerned with the Christian's response to vital issues in

the secular city, Cox turns his attention to work, sex, and learning. He advocates the deliverance of work from religious sanction, a hangover of the "Protestant ethic" in the age of cybernation involving a decrease of jobs and an abundance of leisure. He urges the liberation of sex by an evangelical ethic, from romantic self-deception and commercial exploitation by the "cult of the girl" and the cult of the *Playboy*. He stimulates the Christian to form a reconciling community in service to the university of the secular city. With regard to the church on the campus, Cox engages in a bit of self-laceration about ecclesiastical organization. He seems reluctant to trust ecclesiastical bureaucracy with the same sympathy he gives to the massive bureaucratic developments in the secular city. Perhaps Cox suffers too much from continuing discouragement among religious sociologists over such institutions to offer a fresher challenge to Christians to control their own bureaucracies for Christ's sake. With regard to work, Cox's treatment of the "Protestant ethic" should not be accepted as the final word on the famous Weber thesis about vocation. With regard to sex, Cox's analysis is not intended to be an invitation to promiscuity.

Some of Cox's presuppositions call for further examination. It is one thing to celebrate urbanization, warm to its delights, warn of its dangers, and urge the Christian to accept its disciplines. It is another thing to present to the world a Christian apologetic for secularization on Christian grounds. This reviewer would like to raise two problems.

In the first place, Cox seems to reject myth and metaphysics. Then he shrouds the secular city in a sociological mystique. In dealing with history, for example, Cox warns against discussing "*the* meaning of history." He maintains that his own analysis is not "sequential" and that it is certainly "open-ended." Yet Cox describes history as a "process of secularization" and then proceeds to demonstrate this process with some questionable schematization. On the one hand, he indicates a movement from the tribe, bound by mythology, to the town, bound by metaphysics, to the technopolis, free from myth and metaphysics and presided over by its teams of functioning-pragmatic technopolitans. At one place, Cox asserts that it took two millennia to realize an inclusive metropolis, the inclusiveness presumably an aspect of secularization. Thus there seems to be a progress of man from tribe and town to maturation and an assumption of responsibility in the city. To be sure, Cox assures the reader that the people of the "tribal and town epochs" did encounter the "true God" of the Bible even though they encountered Him within the world views and meaning images of their representative eras. On the other hand, Cox does not explain satisfactorily why the process of secularization should have started in tribal and mobile Israel and should have been disclosed most fully in the good which came out of Nazareth, that obscure town in the Roman Empire of mighty cities. On the basis of Cox's presentation, would it be possible to say that there may be a secular tribe or a secular town? And what difference does it make to the secular city that contemporary man will encounter God within the world view and meaning images of the present time? This historical aspect of Cox's argument discloses that even the most gifted seers in the secular city have trouble with the problem of continuity.

A still more basic question rises in dealing with the place of Jesus of Nazareth in the secular city. Cox says much about Jesus of Nazareth, in whose life God discloses in the fullest possible manner His partnership with man. He interprets Chalcedon in this perspective and introduces an I–You relationship which does justice to the teamwork between God and man. This teamwork is brought about in a purgative process in which the hindrances to mature and responsible action are eliminated.

Two matters are not clear in this connection, however. Does the catharsis for urban man come from the technological developments, the "radical alteration of the environment of the social cataleptic," or from the radical encounter with God in Jesus of Nazareth? This question arises acutely when Cox suggests that traders and adventurers, missionaries and revolutionaries have borne the "seeds of secularization" and started the liberating process of secularization around the world. The Bible does not deny that all men—tribesmen, townsmen, and citified men—may discern God's acts. All

men are without excuse despite the Fall, an Old Testament
category which Cox neglects. But it does illustrate vividly that
men hesitate to accept God's wisdom and power in the weakness and foolishness of Jesus of Nazareth and Christ cruci-
fied.

This leads to the other question. Why does Cox neglect
coming to terms with the biblical emphasis upon the Crucifixion? He holds that history does not take place between the
"black noon of Good Friday and the bright dawn of Easter,"
but between Easter and the Last Day. The emphasis on
Easter as the victory is significant. But Cox is so optimistically busy emphasizing man's maturity and responsibility,
man's work with God, that he neglects the Crucifixion, which
exposes man's rejection of what Cox calls God's partnership
with men and God's work for man. From this analysis of *The
Secular City* there arises no ambiguous and anguished cry:
"O wretched man that I am, who shall deliver me from the
body of this death?" Certainly secularization as openness, not
ideology, and the maturity of the Christian man must come
from an awareness of the misery as well as the grandeur of
man's achievement and an ultimate dependence upon God's
continual forgiveness.

New maturity and a new measure of responsibility are
demanded of Christians who are sons and heirs of God, citizens of the secular city. Cox makes this clear and demonstrates his own possession of these qualities in writing about
one of the most disturbing problems of our day, secularization. After reading this volume, no Christian should handle
the term "secular" casually and exploit it for pious purposes.
Cox states his case vigorously and sometimes brilliantly. This
reviewer finds him sometimes volatile, neglecting because of
his selectivity categories of the Bible which are essential in
any examination of his subject. But for his invigorating challenge, all Christians should be grateful.

# CHAPTER 2

# A Look at the Secular City

## James M. Gustafson

Harvey Cox's book has been so widely circulated, so passionately discussed, and so enthusiastically endorsed that another review seems superfluous. *Christianity and Crisis* devoted an entire issue to the book, and *The New York Times* indicated that in Paul Lehmann's judgment Cox is the Reinhold Niebuhr of this generation. Certainly Cox writes with unusual verve, with pungency of language, with apt use of quoted and paraphrased materials from a phenomenally broad range of sources. What he has written down has been "in the air" for some years; other writers have made many of the same points, but no one has put them all together with such persuasive use of language. Seldom have so many complicated problems been presumably solved in so few pages. Cox is not the author of tedious monographs that win tenure in modern universities, but an extraordinarily intelligent, well-informed synthesizer with all the flair of a publicist. There is a place for such in the economy of the church's mission, but to more bucolic and prosaic academicians some significant questions and reflections remain unresolved.

My impression is that Cox views the church as something that is suffering from isolation, that is chiefly at fault because it is not deeply enough engaged in the world. At this stage of his writing his polemic is primarily addressed to Christians, to the church, passionately pleading with them to give up their old and apparently self-interested ways. He has not yet addressed the "secular" with anything that will help urban mayors, school superintendents, civil-rights leaders, businessmen, and others in the resolution of their moral, technical problems. He is very careful to indicate that there are exceptions to his indictment against the church here and there, and thus properly takes the sting out of some potential criticisms. But it is still fair to ask whether Cox sees the situation of the church correctly. The answer in my judgment is yes and no. All of us who have been loving critics of what has happened to the Christian movement in the world are aware of excessive concern for institutional success, for residential parishes and the like. Insofar as Cox has this in view he is partly correct in his perception.

But some questions can be asked. Does not the pastoral function of the church increase, together with its moral functions, in the dislocations of secularization? The persistent crises of death, broken families, loss of a sense of self, with their morally and spiritually sickening effects also come into the mission of the church and require a reconciling, healing personal ministry. Cox allows for this, but gives it little dignity.

Does Cox do justice to the marks of renewal in the churches, granted their limitations? The ecclesiastical bureaucracies he dislikes have been means for mobilizing resources of money and personnel to man the church's engagement in cities and racial struggles, in industry and slums. It has never been clear to me what the functional equivalents to ecclesiastical institutions are going to be in the new age when these presumed monsters have withered away. Parish churches, under theologically informed, morally sensitive, intelligent leadership have certainly been places of spiritual and moral renewal from which marks of new life have been made in the world.

But these things sound defensive and actually are not the important questions about the church. There are two more that disturb me. First, Cox is prepared to admit that the secular is full of moral ambiguity; he is reluctant to pull all the stops in the organ of praise for the world. But God can use the morally ambiguous secular sphere for His bringing in the Kingdom. If this is the case, cannot the morally ambiguous in the church also be a means of God's action in and for persons, and in and for the world? Behind Cox and others there lurks a somewhat "sectarian" view of the church, not in the sense that the church is to be separated from the world, but in the sense that it is expected to portray the marks of purity and holiness in a way that frees it from critical attack. But surely Saint Paul proclaimed the forgiveness of the sins of the church as well as the redemption of the world, and surely the power that can use the secular to bring in the Kingdom is not powerless to bring new life into the churches —even in their institutionalization. The faith of Christians, like the reign of God in the world, can have visible human forms.

Second, one wonders whether the process of how God's power engenders the Christian prophets and reconcilers is not shortcutted by Cox and by others. Where was my "conscience" nourished, my moral passion kindled, my sense of direction toward a coming Kingdom of God formed? Where was this done for Cox, and for others? In a "Christian" family and a "Christian" church, I must answer for myself. The faith that is made visible in the modern saints' activities in cities did not come to them out of the blue; its soil was tended by parents against whose inadequacies we fulminate, by ministers whose piety we ridicule, by Sunday-school lessons whose emptiness we excoriate, by worship of God, whose name we now believe should be left unspoken. Do we not have to tend to life in the church to bring each generation to an awareness of the Kingdom it is called to serve? These are uninspiring comments, I am sure, but not all the work of the formation of the secular city is any more inspiring, I am equally sure.

The major issue in the book, however, is none of these. It is a theological one, and it has more facets than can be dealt with in this review. The theology of the book is closer to the theological ethics of Paul Lehmann than any other particular writer in America. Christians are "to discern the action of God in the world and to join in His work." For a sweeping generalization, there is nothing wrong with this. The issues come in the refinements, and on this score Cox has not helped us much as yet. Surely everything that is occurring in the world is not completely under the domination of God's purposes. Although there are signs in Cox and other writers that Christ's Lordship is almost identified with what issues from major events of certain kinds in the world, he does not want to claim that the Kingdom is present in everything. Cox comes close to saying that wherever there is revolutionary change going on in the world, there Christ is reigning. Is the Kingdom absent wherever there is not a revolutionary change going on? Is this an implication? Do we write "theologies of social change"? Do we make theology an ideology providing acceptable reasons for participating in forces that are occurring in society of which we happen to approve? Precisely this effort needs closer scrutiny. There have been theologies of tyranny, theologies of reform, theologies of reaction, theologies of revolution, and theologies of most other human impulses. What is revolutionary in our age— secularization and urbanization in Cox's interpretation—will be superseded by other social changes, just as what was revolutionary in other times has been superseded. Surely change is not the only mark of the presence of the Kingdom. One aspires through change to find a juster, better order of life. As that is achieved, is God less present? What is, I believe, intended to be an ethic of "Christ transforming culture" slips easily into an ethic of "Christ of Culture," to use H. R. Niebuhr's types.

If, however, we take seriously the fact that God is not social change or humanization and is not unambiguously ruling in social change, then are we not forced to be more self-critical about the ends, the means, the responses that we make in the world? Discerning what God is doing is a much more complicated task than Cox suggests. It requires a refinement of discrimination rather than broadside hyperbole.

Perhaps I read what is the case in the church incorrectly, but it appears to me that what Christians need is some assistance in finding their way in and through their involvement in secularization and other forces of current society. Surely most Christians are already highly secularized in Cox's sense. Given space, one could take Cox on with reference to sex, universities, and other things in the light of this concern.

As a dispassionate colleague of mine is wont to say when

he reads a stirring book, "It's exciting, but is it accurate?" But John Fry in *The Immobilized Christian* has already answered that question by in effect asking academic ethicians another question: "It may be academically respectable and refined, but has it ever moved anyone?" In the economy of the church's mission, perhaps we need both.

# CHAPTER 3

# How Do We Speak of God Without Religion?

*Bernard Murchland*

It is difficult to speak of God when He is presumed dead. But Harvey Cox makes a noteworthy attempt. He by no means succeeds in extricating himself from the numerous difficulties involved; nonetheless, he has written a valuable book. It is not highly original or exceptionally profound, but it is relevant and encompassing. And if it is not always convincing, it is consistently stimulating. In these days of theological upheaval *The Secular City* is something to be grateful for. It indicates, among other things, that a spark of the ancient fire still smolders.

In general terms the book tries to answer the problem raised by Dietrich Bonhoeffer, who wrote from a Nazi prison camp in 1944, "How do we speak of God without religion? How do we speak in a secular fashion of God?" There can be no doubt, Cox argues with crepitating insistence, that we must indeed speak of Him in a secular fashion. The religion of Western Christendom, with its reliance on mythical and metaphysical categories, is gone forever. The old transcendent structure has collapsed. . . .

That secularization is a fact, and has been for some time, few will dispute. But secularization is not only a fact; it is a desirable fact. Furthermore, Cox argues, secularization "represents an authentic consequence of biblical faith." Creation marks a new state of religious awareness; it signals a departure from the enchantment of magic and animism. The Genesis narratives distinguish between the orders of God, man, and nature. Adam becomes co-responsible with God for the created order. Man has been given a mandate to assume responsibility for his world. Cox finds further justification for secularization by examining the biblical accounts of the Exodus and Mount Sinai. . . .

Against this scriptural backdrop, Cox elaborates his analysis of the secular city and investigates the possibilities of Christian growth within it. Society today is characterized by anonymity and mobility; its style is at once pragmatic and profane (as illustrated by John F. Kennedy and Albert Camus, respectively). Not a few well-intentioned moralists have bemoaned the plight of man in such a society: his facelessness, his depersonalization, his alienation. But Cox thinks this has been a misdirected effort. It represents a failure to confront the world as it is. . . .

There is something plausible about this line of argument. It is particularly good to hear a theological voice in a constructive register endeavoring to make some sense out of our present situations and dilemmas. But there is something puzzling about it as well. I should say Cox's analysis is accurate enough. But it is too glib, too uncritical. For one thing, he rather too readily overlooks the alienating effects of the secular city, its great power to victimize. The advent of the alienated man, C. W. Mills has pointed out, "and all the themes which lie behind his advent now affect the whole of our serious intellectual life and cause our immediate intellectual malaise. I know of no idea, no theme, no problem that . . . is so much involved in the possible default of contemporary social science."

Cox conveniently ignores a powerful body of sociological criticism (since Marx), as well as a significant phychological critique that has been building since the time of Freud. In my opinion his case simply cannot stand until it comes to terms with such criticism. And how would he cope with the testimony of modern literature and art? There is no way around the negativity engendered by the secular city. There may be a way through it, but Cox does not elect this route.

One can, of course, make theological sense of some kind out of any given predicament. Thus Cox manages rather well in blessing his secular city and all its works with appropriate biblical texts. But he does so at the cost of suppressing equally relevant biblical data. The same Genesis narrative that establishes man's responsibility for the created order also speaks of his fall, of man's perennial tendency to slip away from the desirable ideal. Just as Cox largely ignores the alienation in society, so too he fails to take sufficiently into account its theological cognate, which usually goes by the name of sin. Pragmatism has not yet proven itself capable of dealing with either form of negativity in any convincing way.

Perhaps, at bottom, this is a failure of methodology. Cox looks first to the situation, to what is going on, and then follows with a theological justification. The problem here is that there is no guarantee that what is there calls for such justification. This is a fallacy of functionalism that has in recent history led us up all sorts of blind alleys—Hitler's wars, for example. Such a method lacks an adequate critical principle. What men as a matter of fact do certainly has some bearing on the ethical question of what they ought to do. But it is not the whole picture. The facts of human life are after all functions of our ideals and not vice versa.

Thus, when Cox argues that "the grammar of the Gospel is not a categorical imperative; it first of all points to what *is* occurring, only secondarily does it call for a consequent change in attitude and action" (p. 116)* he is surely wrong. The Gospel is full of imperatives of one sort or another. Commandments are laid down; attitudes are inculcated; perfection is demanded. In particular the evangelical ideals of love and justice are recommended as possible states, before any corresponding embodiment of these ideals is expected contextually. The point of the Gospel is not so much to put man on his own, as Cox would have it; rather, its dynamism derives from its manner of situating man within a larger, and indeed transcendent, context of creativity. Only in this way can we make any sense out of grace and such transforming virtues as suffering and patience, traditional categories Cox pays far too little heed to. In fact, only in this way can we fully justify the maturation and responsibility he repeatedly urges.

A similar problem arises with Cox's identification of the

---

* The page references throughout are to the paperback edition.

Kingdom of God with the secular city. The question is not self-validating. There is a kind of reductionism here that lacks a purifying criterion. It is true, of course, as it is desirable, that we can dispense with Augustinian dualism. A long-standing and very pernicious kind of supernaturalism is rightly exorcised. And Cox is astutely theological when he writes, "The Kingdom of God, concentrated in the life of Jesus of Nazareth, remains the fullest possible disclosure of the partnership of God and man in history. Our struggle for the shaping of the secular city represents the way we respond faithfully to this reality in our own times" (p. 112). Neverthe-less, there is an element of question begging here. Just what kind of city we ought to be shaping remains unclear. To say, as Cox does, that the secular city is a historical process which removes adolescent illusions is simply naïve. Our age is as beleaguered by illusion and superstition as any other. And Cox's own remarks in his chapter on sex (an excellent one it is too) and elsewhere in the book indicate that he himself is aware of this.

Reinhold Niebuhr once noted that the orthodox churches are inclined to petrify the Christian message with the insights and attitudes of a past age. The liberal religions, on the other hand, tend to compromise too readily with the passing preju-dices of a particular culture. "The failure of liberal Chris-tianity," Niebuhr says, "is derived from its inclination to in-vest the relative moral standards of a commercial age with ultimate sanctity by falsely casting the aura of the absolute and transcendent ethic of Jesus upon them. A religion which capitulates to the prejudices of a contemporary age is not very superior to a religion which remains enslaved to the partial and relative insights of an age already dead." This seems an indisputably valid criticism. And I fear that, to some extent at least, Professor Cox is guilty of it. He strains too hard, if not at a gnat, at least at a society that in itself is transitory. The concept of the secular city can bear only so much theological freight.

I found the best part of the book to be the author's discus-sion of the church as God's avant-garde, as a people whose collective activities should lead them to a participation in

God's action in the world. He sees the church's role as four-fold. First, its kerygmatic function, the broadcasting of its message, which is, as Cox sees it, the defeat of "principalities and powers"—which in secular terms indicates the various cultural forces which militate against human freedom. In reference to an earlier criticism, let me note that the author does not seem sufficiently cognizant that the secular city itself may be such a force.

Secondly, there is the church's diakonic function, its effort to impart wholeness and health. In political terms, it means a radical confrontation of our grievous social ailments, with obvious shades of the earlier Social Gospel movement.

Thirdly, the church exercises a koinoniac role. It proclaims the signs of the Kingdom to the world, "harbingers of a reality which is breaking into history not from the past but from the future" (p. 147).

Finally, the church functions as a cultural exorcist, freeing men from the "narcotic vagaries through which they wrongly perceive the social reality around them, and from habitual forms of action or inaction stemming from these illusions."

The issue of God is left somewhat unresolved. Cox thinks by and large that we ought to speak of Him in a political manner, for politics is "the sphere of human mastery and responsibility," "the living lexicon of the urban-secular man." Here again, his inveterate reductionism intrudes. Politics will in this new age do what metaphysics once did. Theologically, about all we can say of God is that He is hidden. We meet Him "at those places in life where we come up against that which is not pliable and disposable, at those hard edges where we are both stopped and challenged to move ahead. God meets us as the transcendent, at those aspects of our experience which can never be transmuted into extensions of ourselves. He meets us in the wholly other" (p. 262). I fear to think what a linguistic analyst might do with a passage like that! It may be too that we shall have to get rid of the word "God" and rename Him. The new name will be determined by our historical conditions and meanings; it will be a function of our new experiences of freedom. Meanwhile, Cox suggests, perhaps not without a touch of irony, it might be well to take a moratorium on speech until the new name emerges.

I have entered some strong reservations about *The Secular City*. But I should like to conclude in a more positive tone. The book, to my mind, is an excellent prolegomenon to what has been called a theology of terrestrial values, with the emphasis on social ethics. Perhaps it would have been a better book if it were more person, rather than event, centered. But no matter. If Cox's sociological analyses are sometimes skimpy and if his theological prehension is frequently adumbrative, he has nonetheless performed one remarkable service: he has in a very comprehensive way directed theological discourse to the arena of social action and historical process where the Spirit is at work. It has been too long absent from that domain.

A whole theological reconstruction is necessary in our day (as the Vatican Council, among other evidences, has made clear), and much of what Cox says can aid us in that arduous task. He has grasped an important demension of theological investigation and has described for us in some detail the kind of world that theology must come to terms with. Whether or not his own theology does so is another question.

The philosophical disciplines have preceded theology in this work. Most of the major schools of the past century have attempted a critique of our theories about the world (including the world of God) in terms of the world directly encountered. And the world directly encountered, as John Randall has said, "is found to be fundamentally temporal in character, to be specific and plural, a many rather than a neat one, to be capable of inquiry and manipulation in detail, to be subject to experimental reconstruction and to be fundamentally functional in character, an affair of many specific means-ends relations." Perhaps American naturalism, more than any other school, has contributed to this vision. Harvey Cox is firmly within that naturalistic tradition and the consequences for theology could be very significant.

# CHAPTER 4

# Supercity

## from *Christianity Today*

Bishop John Robinson and his followers might well look to their laurels, for another prophet has risen that could throw them into obscurity. Harvey Cox is a Baptist crying loudly in the modern secular world. He leaves existentialism in his dust and outruns the demythologizing Bultmannians, envisioning a new era in human history emerging from the secularization of life.

In his book *The Secular City*, Cox writes about "technopolis." He maintains that the old tribal society and the later town culture have vanished. Supercity is at hand—the metropolis of automation, mass communication, mobility, and anonymity. The up-to-date technopolitans are not concerned with the antiquated mysteries of religion. They have no use for the hereafter. For them this world affords sufficient problems without bothering about the Beyond.

Cox is certain that the world has become "defatalized." "God" is a meaningless term to secularized minds. The world task is man's, not the Lord's. In fact, we should quit talking about God. Nobody is listening anyhow. "Reconciliation" is still a meaningful word; God is breaking through in secular events and movements. It is up to the church to "identify" with these events and thus to become the Lord's avant-garde at this point in history. We must lift our eyes from the past to the future. Worship at 11 A.M. is but a remnant of the farm schedule with a gap between milking hours. Sermons belong to an outdated era when leaders discoursed to those who were forbidden to talk back.

Cox suggests that we consider the primitive church. What

gave it such an impetus into history? The forward look. Today we are looking backward. Those early Christians, he asserts, eagerly anticipated the coming again of the Lord, and this caused them to concentrate earnestly on the future. We modern believers must also forget the past. We must not only renovate our theological language but also restructure our message. Such old ideas as that of God as a Father, or even a Supreme Being, must be discarded. We must talk this-world talk. The secularized society demands a pragmatic advance into the future. And this is no small task. We should eliminate the meaningless word "God." Nobody knows what it means any more. New expressions for our faith must be invented; new terms acceptable to the new secularistic mind must be used. We must get busy "liberating the captives," sure in our faith that we will find a new name for God as well as a new religion.

Many obscurantist, behind-the-times evangelicals may, of course, be gratified that Professor Cox commends these early disciples of Christ for being avant-garde in their particular moment in history. When the author of *The Secular City* reminds us that the first Christians looked forward in earnest expectation to the end of the age and the coming again of the Lord, one wonders if he is aware of how many evangelical obscurantists today have that same forward look toward the same event anticipated by the early church. True, we look back to Calvary and the resurrection of Christ. Yet we also, even in the celebration of communion, "show the Lord's death till he come."

Actually, evangelicals look farther into the future than Professor Cox. They see, beyond supercities and technopolitan goings-on, beyond man's present confusion and international wranglings and warrings, a world where "the wolf shall dwell with the lamb." They look to the day when the name we are asked to forget shall be praised "from the rising of the sun unto the going down of the same," to the time when the Son of Man, who in the past was lifted up on a cross, will return to establish his kingdom.

They look to a "supercity" whose builder and ruler is God, where "the tabernacle of God is with men, and He will dwell with them, and they shall be His people, and God Himself shall be with them, and be their God." In that supercity, freed from the cynicism of human technopolitans, men will do more than mention the name of God; they will make it sound like a symphony.

# CHAPTER 5

# Today's City: Threat or Promise?

*Max L. Stackhouse*

That rapid urbanization has become a worldwide phenomenon, with new metropolitan centers of population appearing everywhere, is widely recognized. But that the city has attained symbolic and moral power among the world's people is not so widely acknowledged. The city is the symbol of progress, excitement, and freedom from drudgery; it is also the symbol of moral decadence, oppression and loss of authentic identity. The variety of possible interpretations of the city is matched only by the multifaceted character of urban life. Among the many possible interpretations, however, three contemporary efforts have particular significance for the major conflicts and disputes of modern life. While many aspects of urban life are more subtly and more accurately represented in technical works, the Communist, Catholic and sectarian Protestant branches of modern culture have all recently produced documents that may well have long-range consequences.

The most radical and revolutionary branch of modern culture, that which has captured the East through a fundamentalist, agrarian millennialism, is best represented by an article in the *Peking Review* (No. 36, September 3, 1965, pp. 9–30). Marshal Lin Piao, China's defense minister, there sets forth his interpretation of modern history and calls on the world's people to join China in a war to destroy "United States imperialism." A key metaphor on which he bases his interpretation and his recommended strategy is the conflict between the countryside and the city. Not only does Lin Piao try to capitalize on the perennial myth of the moral inferiority of the city and the hostility of the "pure, simple folk" toward city slickers, not only does his article reflect Communist China's revolutionary experience under the cry of agrarian reform, but the thesis he sets forth becomes the basis for his picture of the entire world situation. The city, he writes, is the seat of the "imperialists," who "usually begin by seizing the main lines of communication." In contrast,

> The countryside is the seat of the real people who protect the world from the imperialists who always try to exploit them. . . . The countryside, and the countryside alone, can provide the revolutionary bases from which the revolutionary forces can go forward to victory. . . . Taking the entire globe, if North America and Western Europe can be called the "cities of the world," then Asia, Africa and Latin America constitute the "rural areas of the world." . . . In a sense, the contemporary world revolution also presents a picture of the encirclement of cities by rural areas.

Marx and Lenin had contempt for rural life, and any honest reading of the Marxist literature would show that the expected leaders of the world's revolution were to be the urban proletariat, the industrial workers—not the rural peoples. Yet here, under the claims of an absolute logic and of a mechanical destiny in history, we find an interpretation directed against the city and all that urban citizenship represents.

A highly contrasting conservative view is represented by the letter sent June 21, 1965, on behalf of Pope Paul VI by Amleto Cardinal Cicognani, papal secretary of state, to the president of the French *Semaines Sociales*. Hardly representative of the kind of sensitivity among the Roman Catholic community that the world has been led to expect by Vatican II, it nevertheless illustrates a type of symbolic and moral interpretation of the city that is held by many religious persons who have not realized that Christendom is no longer the principle of modern social organization. Cardinal Cicognani points out that "absolute and permanent values, closely linked to human nature and in a necessary relation with the

supernatural end of the person," are threatened by urbanization, "the extent of which radically modifies the traditional
way of life of families, shatters the structure of society and is
not without grave consequences for the social adjustment of
individuals and of families and for their religious behavior."
The letter urges participants in the *Semaines* to seek ways of
"not only safeguarding [these ultimates] but possibly
strengthening them in the midst of the revolutionary
changes." Further, "no structural evolution, no more than
any temporal organization, can legitimately put [them] in
question."

Although the papal letter recognizes effects of urbanization
and city life as "the sign, the cause and effect of a radical
transformation in society and a profound change in human
psychology," it does not consider them capable of modifying
or compromising the eternal truths taught by the Catholic
Church. Thus urbanization is a historical epiphenomenon to
which eternity must speak, an epiphenomenon which, with
possible promise if kept under the guidance of right reason,
nevertheless bears the dangers of "anarchy," "banalization of
thought," "depersonalization of man," "anonymity" and "ag-
glomerations of solitude."

One senses below the surface of the letter a fear of heterogeneity, differentiation and pragmatic techniques, linked with
a preference for organic wholeness, harmony and integrity
for society—an establishment governed, much on the model
of the Greek *polis,* by and for spiritual and rational man on
his way to a heavenly City of God.

A third interpretation of the city is best represented by a
tractarian paperback from a sectarian Protestant perspective.
Not, of course, having the authoritative imprimatur of the
other views, it has, by popular acclaim, become the handbook
of large segments of Protestant clergy, bureaucrats and laity,
not to mention some progressive Catholics. Harvey Cox's *The
Secular City* sees *in*—not over or under or around or against
—the technological secular civilization represented by the
modern city a vision of man's possibilities and a potential
fulfillment of the promises reality makes to man.

As a summary expression of the realistic view of history
linked with a profound social conscience, this book captures

much of the wisdom of the Social Gospel; the fruits of the
realist movement in the theology of the 1930s; some of the
genius of crisis theology; and the experience of a generation
born in the Depression, raised during World War II and the
cold war, grown to manhood under radioactive clouds—all
without losing hope. It is governed by a pragmatic and provisional hope coupled with a cautious, even taciturn, faith. Yet
it is a real hope and a real faith capable of finding solace in
the freeing power of computers as well as fear of their potential bondage, capable of finding beauty as well as terror in a
rocket, capable of seeing a new humanity attempting to rise
from the ashes of race riots as well as the agony of destruction.

*The Secular City* is written with an art that betrays the
author's free-church, Baptist background, both in his charismatic spirit and in his ingenious use of Scripture—a use
only a few steps removed from proof-texting to seal and
secure each point. Cox's background sometimes leads him
into difficulty. Although he recognizes the importance of
bureaucracy for work, he frequently succumbs to the free-
church suspicion of institutionalized forms of renewal while
at the same time celebrating the power of technology to in-
duce positive change. He thereby fails to see that technology
is historically and constitutionally dependent on the ability to
mobilize and organize large numbers of people into interdependent work units. Yet his bias more often permits him to
cut himself and modern man free from the burden of Lin
Piao's "*the* natural logic of history" and of Cardinal Cicognani's "the absolute and permanent values" and to affirm a
pragmatic, historically sensitive interpretation of human existence.

Indeed, the whole point of the accent on the secular world
Cox calls us to celebrate is that modern man can find provisional but significant meaning in a world where nature no
longer has mystical symbolic power (we have to decide what
we are going to do with it rather than letting it tell us what to
do); where politics is no longer sacramentalized; and where
the values that integrate our lives are not necessarily located
in doctrines and church creeds, or even secular ideologies.

Serious problems arise in relation to the later portions of

the book. Does not Cox's treatment of sex lead to a somewhat romanticized remythologization of the sex act rather
than the functional-realist view earlier portions of the book
lead one to expect? And does not the image of the Kingdom
of God in his hands cause a rebaptism of the very political
order that he has taken considerable pains to secularize? And
why does the sensitive treatment of most human relations
seem to crumble into a moribund I–Thou understanding of
the church when it could have assumed its most forceful and
clearest conceptualization?

In spite of these and other difficulties, I believe that Protestant theologians of the contemporary mold will find the
burden of proof on them when they dissociate themselves
from the main *intentions* of the book, for in many ways it is
a highly readable, even popular, rendering of the conclusions
and inclinations of the best American theology of the past
century. Whether it will stand the test of years cannot now be
determined, but that it is worthy of immediate discussion is
clear.

That is my purpose here. But rather than rehearsing the
book's contents further (it would be tragic to give so much of
it that people would try to talk about it without wrestling
with it themselves), I propose to raise some preliminary questions and make some suggestions that follow on Dr. Cox's
conclusions.

It is important to note that the authors of all three documents use the term "city" as a symbol of modern culture.
They are talking not about such problems of the city as urban
sprawl, road construction, election campaigns and water supplies but about a way to conceive of and evaluate styles of
life, sets of values, ranges of hopes and expectations, coteries
of preferences and strategies that are implied in or are a
prerequisite for urban life. Thus the city is not a city, but
"the city," symbol of contemporary urban (modern bourgeois, if you will) culture. But an interpretation of the city
cannot be valid if it demands destruction of that which it also
promises, as does the statement of Lin Piao. Indeed, one can
even ask whether it is possible to engage in a theological
interpretation of the city in view of the discontinuity between

the terms of the interpretation and the object of interpretation.

An interpretation of modern urban culture presupposes several things about theology and about culture. In the first place, it is assumed that theology can speak to a historical situation which it did not anticipate, out of a context that it knows nothing about, and indeed has frequently resisted the particular historical situations that now obtain. In spite of Cox's attempt to pull the cloak of theological respectability about the process of secularization by ingenuous reference to particular passages of Scripture and eisegetic use of traditional doctrines, we must be cautious about attempts to move from biblical or traditional views to a modern, urban, secular view of man, existence and society—or from here to there. The character of our historical consciousness is at stake. And it is different aspects of our historical consciousness that both binds us to, and separates us from our past.

In the second place, it is assumed that a primary obligation of theology is to provide a set of moral guidelines for action in modern history.

Both of these assumptions about theology are valid, but only if we admit several presuppositions. If theology is seen as a body of holy truths that need only to be spelled out, then a theology of urban culture is not possible. Our continuity with the saints of previous ages and with what distinguishes them and us as Christians is not, I think, at the level of assent to already defined eternal and holy truths. H. Richard Niebuhr has pointed out that we do not have absolute ideas; we have only ideas of the absolute. And these ideas change.  Theology must therefore be seen as a historical process of continual adoption and adaptation of symbols and meanings taken from the dynamic movement of historical events, just as the New Testament may be seen as a series of attempts to interpret what was going on in the lives of Jesus and his followers and in the historical tendencies of the time.

Thus man speaks theologically when he attempts to define the ethos of which he is part in its normative aspects and in terms of its whence and whither. Men who attempt to do this are under the direct or indirect influence of Christ,

whether they explicitly confess him or not. The kind of historical consciousness that permits man to look at history as a
locus of radical personal and institutional involvement, commitment and meaning comes only from the claim that the
nearest thing to ultimate reality man can know appears in the
midst of human history, with its joy and tragedy, partial
successes and partial failures. Natural man, on the contrary,
always looks to the cosmos, the gods and metaphysics. But
modern man, the man of the secular city, is a participant in a
peculiar, quite unnatural, quite antimystical, quite antimetaphysical setting that can be seen only as either threatening
total alienation from reality or portending a promising, if
unfulfilled, historically mediated grace. An adequate theology
of urban culture must hold to the latter position.

The fact that theology as a process *can* speak to and from
the urban secular setting does not necessarily mean that it
*ought* to do so. Yet religion (and the theological enterprise
generally) obtains and sustains its legitimacy through its ethical power, which is related to but not totally dependent on its
intellectual acuity. Thus the vitality of Christianity decreases
proportionately to its lack of relevance. Ethical power—that
is, the ability to provide the means for the definition, the
criticism, the transformation and, where possible, the vindica-
tion of the ethos—is the necessary basis for a theology
today.

A theological interpretation of urban culture also presupposes several things about culture. It claims that culture is
susceptible of theological analysis; that a given culture has
pervasive characteristics that can be identified and dealt with;
that there is within each culture sufficient tension between
positive and negative values that the theological effort never
either becomes totally against culture or is swallowed by it.
The polarity of Christ against culture on the one hand and
Christ identified with culture on the other becomes a false
dichotomy.

For all that one may wish to echo Cox's criticism of the
ontologism of Paul Tillich, the lack of appreciation of his
pioneering in the whole area of the theology of culture borders on the scandalous. For Tillich made this book possible
more than any other contemporary theologian by teaching

that cultural phenomena are such that one can speak from and to man's historically conditioned cultural involvement and find in it matters of ultimate concern. Values of both a positive and a negative sort are built into the cultural and social setting, and it is less a question of adding God to the ethos or posing God against the ethos as it is a question of finding where in the ethos God is at work sustaining, maintaining, transforming, vindicating and judging, and of finding where powers, structures, hardened hearts and self-celebrating persons and groups are inhibiting the fulfillment of all His promises.

If the preceding paragraphs have any validity, theology becomes a critical development of changing hypothetical models or frameworks by which the ethos may be analyzed. But what are the crucial factors in the urban ethos and what are the theological ideas that can serve as a modern model for an analysis and transformation of our ethos?

The city, the modern setting of man, is an artifact. It is made, not given. Although it could not be made without the given, that which is significant about it is that which is made, not that which is given. Living in an environment of his own creation, modern urban man can only with difficulty and some dishonesty maintain the old principles of human solidarity, social stability and historical continuity. Thus some variety of synergism is necessary. Man is an important ingredient in the creating and sustaining of the conditions that make life meaningful.

The city is also the locus of change and differentiation. Dr. Cox suggests the direction in which theology may well move if it is to develop a theology of change and revolution to deal with the catapulting events of modern life. And he does it in a way that makes change an exciting adventure rather than that vision of a plummeting decay portrayed by many modern writers who want to sound prophetic but usually show themselves to be merely victims of misplaced nostalgia. But can we have only change? Do we not need to take account of the relative stability institutions provide, preventing the chaos of change alone, and to find ways in which structural change can be implemented?

Dr. Cox also portrays the values and potential virtues in

pluralism. In order to assert their common humanity people need not have all the same ideas, be of the same religion, belong to a given racial group or even stand at the same level on the social-cultural-economic scale. Heterogeneity provides a richness in community life that is invaluable, and anonymity sometimes frees us from the oppressive power of the law. But in a pluralistic urban society people need some sort of community life to stand between the highly personal I–Thou relationship and the impersonal consensus of mass politics besides the interest group of union, professional association or corporation. People need the personal experience of moral demands that community life makes upon them to keep liberty from becoming license, to keep freedom from the law from becoming anomie, anonymity from becoming alienation.

The Gospel, the kerygma, does not destroy the law; it transforms it. If some intermediate groups and provisional norms are not provided, the "natural" bases of community—national or religious chauvinism, tribalism, class interest—will assert themselves in their full pagan power, as the twentieth century has seen only too well. And no secular, pragmatic interest group can hold them back. Indeed, the perennial urban tensions—city versus suburb, haves versus have-nots, white versus black, Protestant versus Catholic, conservative versus liberal—are present precisely because adequate middle-level institutional centers of identity, righteousness and justice have not been provided. To call for the healing of these breaches avails little unless some alternatives are provided to today's structures. If the made world of urban life is to survive, it must make new centers of social solidarity and stability in which people may participate, with which they may identify, around which new forms of social life may nucleate.

The questions, then, are whether we can find new institutional forms that can accomplish creatively what the present institutions inadequately provide (by necessity but also by default), and whether those forms can avoid becoming self-idolatrous. Or, to put it at another level, the question is whether theologians, especially theological ethicists and theologians of culture, can find an adequate set of concepts to help create and sustain the required institutions. A subsidiary question follows: Can the theological-ethical notion of "covenant" provide the model for such social solidarity?

Cox's idea of the church as God's avant-garde is very suggestive. It contains several ingredients needed to construct an adequate model for the new social forms required by modern urban life. It has a charismatic, prophetic character that recognizes the importance of "commitment" and "involvement." It reflects something of the actual experience of pastors who have paid a heavy price for participation in such activities as civil-rights movements. It challenges directly the cultured despisers who see the church as a residue of previous ages. And it suggests the dynamic sensitivity to historical change that reaches toward the *eschaton* that is integral to any sound interpretation of Christianity as a movement.

But what is the church's shape, its structure, its organizational principle? How do you recognize a church without confusing it with the moribund rearguard action of many churches or with flurries of altruistic activism? It is well to describe the church's functions: servant and healer to the city, advocate of the oppressed and exposer of the oppressors— these are some of its most important callings. But what structures are required, what kinds of institutions must be created if it is to play those roles? The structure is not totally a product of the function, for it determines the division of labor and the allocation of resources, hence the limits of function. In short, one would not so much criticize what Cox has said on this question as point to a serious omission: the failure to fill out the notion of the "church as God's avant-garde" by pointing toward organizational possibilities.

"Covenant" has a positive ring among Protestants of the Calvinist and free-church traditions, and it has its possible correlates in some of the recent Catholic thought under the rubric "people of God." What is at stake in these notions must be included in a new ecclesiology if the church is to become God's avant-garde in the modern city and exemplify the new forms of institutional life that can earn it that title. "Covenant" may well be a crucial metaphor for understanding and promoting the formation of new social solidarities not based on ideological, racial or class loyalties.

The concept of the covenant bears within it several possibilities that make it appropriate for modern life. It sees that social forms are made, not given in creation, nature or supernatural idea—even though once created they take on a power and a logic of their own that are not fully manipulatable, in a way that directly fits our experience in modern urban existence.

The covenant provides a structure for morals, for it involves a binding and pledging of mutual responsibilities arrived at by mutual consent. In covenant there is a basis for flexible order and institutionalized change, a path that allows us, as Reinhold Niebuhr has repeatedly warned us, to sail between the twin perils of the Scylla of externalized and formalized rigidity on one side and the Charybdis of chaos and anomie on the other.

Further, the covenant idea bears within it a latent interpretation of history. First, it recognizes that different covenants (or at least different specifications of *the* covenant) obtain in different periods and thus the idea presses us to investigate comparative social settings and to scrutinize our own times to determine what covenantal forms are most appropriate. A relativity is introduced, but not an absolute relativity; for within particular settings are discernible relative stabilities that provide continuity and coherence. Second, not only does the covenant theory speak of various periods of the past and present, but it expects future covenants and the promises of the present to be fulfilled. Both in eschatological expectations and hopes and in hardheaded planning for change there is a tendency to anticipate the new forms that are to be.

Still further, the covenant notion involves not only the formation of particular organizations but also concern for problems, values, groups and persons that extend beyond the covenanting group. Providing the necessary middle-level group organization that serves as a locus of reference and identity, it maintains also a voluntary basis of membership, a corporate discipline and a universal reference.

Finally, covenantal thinking provides a way of thinking

about God that de-emphasizes accent on the "being" of God and emphasizes instead His will, His action and His Kingdom. This points us toward the reality of the modern experience that God is felt, seen or heard not directly but indirectly. This indirection has led some thinkers to speak of the death of God and the silence of God. On the contrary, the metaphor of the covenant recognizes that God's self-revelation is always mediate and that His will can best be discerned where community-forming powers are at work, bringing men and women into new and creative covenants in the midst of a secular world.

In short, that adequate interpretation of the city which must soon be made must be capable of avoiding the absolutisms of Lin Piao and Cardinal Cicognani. Dr. Cox has provided us with the best alternative so far, one that not only brings the church up to date but pioneers some virgin territory. Nevertheless, protests against false absolutisms have led him to disparage form and structure, organization and institution too quickly. An explicit theological ethical concept of the covenant, linked with the historical-eschatological sensitivities present in Cox, can, I believe, provide an organizational principle that can lead to a sustaining and controlling of the revolutionary movements already afoot in the secular cities around the world, movements even now worthy of our interest, our participation and our support.

# CHAPTER 6

# The Secular City and the Bible

## George W. Peck

The task to which Professor Cox calls us is important and significant; the Gospel must be rethought in the face of modernity, science, urbanization, and secularity. The basic point is well taken and disturbingly presented. Many of us have had our heads in the sand too long. But the book professes to be more than just a stimulus. It also seeks to offer us guidelines for our future progress—even tries to lay down quite a bit of the road. And that is where it seems to me to run into difficulties. As a jolt to start us on the journey, it works remarkably effectively, but there are too many unsolved problems of method, too many gaps in the argument, too many rhetorical generalizations, too many examples of biblical, historical, and theological sloppiness for it to succeed as well as we might wish. Our pilgrimage is before us, but where it is to lead and how it is to be fulfilled theologically *The Secular City* does not manage to tell us with complete clarity. There are places where it may even end by being distinctly misleading. This is particularly true, I believe, in regard to the use which it makes of the Bible.

Cox is concerned to a remarkable degree with anchoring his position firmly in the Scriptures, and that is laudable enough. It is the way he does it which must give us pause. Taking the secular city, or the outlook of modern urban man, as his base of operation, he ranges through the Old and New Testaments and fastens now here, now there, upon likely (or unlikely) passages which, with a few deft twists of exegetical analysis, are made to fit neatly into place in the scheme of what our generation is said to be able to believe. Often it is just a little *too* neat. We may not come across a *deus ex machina* in the secular city, but we do appear to have to make a good deal of use of a sort of *Scriptura ex machina* methodology. Time and again Cox sketches an extreme notion of secularized theology which in itself is both striking and suggestive, then disconcerts us by suddenly turning and saying, "But look, it's really all there in the Bible after all." And the impression is repeatedly given that the references thus selected are somehow capable of yielding the meaning being ascribed to them by simple inspection, when in fact this is often clearly not so.

Actually a kind of *ad hoc* process of demythologizing, or spiritualization, or what have you, is going on without our being explicitly told about it and without being supplied with the precise hermeneutical principles on the basis of which the translation or reformulation is being carried out. Certainly some of the passages used are capable of other interpretations than those which Professor Cox happens to favor. Take for instance the discussion of mobile modern man in the light of the Yahweh-Baal conflict (pp. 51ff.). This relationship could perhaps be very helpful as a homiletical device for a rather striking Sunday morning sermon, but it will have difficulty standing up as scientific exegesis. When the Jews (?) were wandering and homeless, we are told, they were closest to fulfilling their calling. Therefore, man today on the throughways of urban society, etc. etc. The Old Testament had already solved the problem of the despatialization of the Deity, and we have only to relearn that lesson in our time for our country-town provincialism to wither away. But was the God of the Old Testament in fact ever completely despatialized? Wasn't he simply in one sense relocated in different spaces from time to time, until finally he was elevated high over all, from which vantage point he could take care of everything and everybody all at once? At least that seems to me a possible way of reading the situation, if the Old Testament is taken simply at its face value. Isn't that the significance of the three-story universe that is such an issue with the Bultmannians? God is pushed upstairs from Horeb, the Ark, and the Temple, until he comes eventually to sit "on the circle of the earth." And isn't it then a problem to get him down into the world again, so that angels and aeons and so forth have to come increasingly into play in the intertestamental and New Testament periods?

What has all that to do with modern man on the throughway? By all means let us argue that it can have a great deal to do with him—but let us first admit that some heavy work is going to have to be done before he is able to see it. How this is to be achieved is the hermeneutical problem, and it is this problem that is given all too scant attention in *The Secular City*. More often than not Cox stops his exegetical investigation before this troublesome matter is even allowed to reveal itself fully. Granted, the story of the naming of the animals in Genesis is intriguing (pp. 73 ff.), but even if the somewhat dubious interpretation which is placed upon it by von Rad is correct, where does that leave us? We may have a God who brings men into partnership with himself in creation—but aren't we still talking also about a God who walks in gardens, has conversations with men, gives them orders, has them name things, and so forth? And isn't that a bit remote from modern, urban, secular man? By what right do we say anything about this charming piece of mythology to our generation at all? And by what critically spelled-out principle(s) of hermeneutics do we extract from the passage an alleged kernel which suits our purpose and reject the remainder because it apparently does not?

Some even more subtle cases of this kind of thing occur when Cox finds his material in the New Testament. It looks like a masterstroke when the concept of "inaugurated eschatology" is discovered in the teaching of Jesus and of the early church and appears to cohere so well with the notion of the secular city as the image of the Kingdom of God (pp. 110 ff.). But what we are not told is that the inaugurated eschatology of the New Testament always (except perhaps in the fourth Gospel if we edit it *à la* Bultmann) looks forward to the not-too-distant coming of Jesus a second time upon clouds of glory to wind up world history in a final cataclysm. *This* is the real problem which any application of New Testament eschatology to modern times has to wrestle with—the possibility of effecting a transition from a world view which saw history as soon to come to a dramatic end to one in which no end is anywhere in sight. Verbally, inaugurated eschatology may look strikingly like the scheme of things in *The Secular City*, but in fact the similarity could turn out to be more apparent than real unless something is done to show why a historical expectation in the first century which did not come to anything can still be regarded as the vehicle for a viable message to a generation two thousand years later. I find it hard to discern where Cox has even touched upon this tricky question.

Exactly the same can be said of a statement like this: "To believe the kerygma is to believe that man not only *should* but *can* 'have dominion over the earth' " (p. 129). Aside from the fact that this sounds remarkably like a return to the facile optimism of a former period, as it stands it is a far cry from the apparent meaning of the New Testament. What the kerygma of the early church seems to me to say rather pointedly is that the *elect* are going to have dominion over the new earth *in the eschaton,* but certainly not "man" in general *in the world here and now.* If we are going to make the sort of shift that Cox brings about (and I entirely agree that some shift is needed), we are surely bound to have to take a little more seriously the hermeneutical problems involved in it. We must be able to explain somewhat more satisfactorily how we are still able to contend that despite the evident differences between our own formulations and those of the Bible we are nonetheless bringing to speech for our time the same word that the first Christians proclaimed to theirs.

On many occasions Cox's style of interpretation reminded me more strongly than anything else of the spiritualizing of the exegetes of the Middle Ages. But the trouble is that what these men were doing was based upon, and quite in accord with, a doctrine of Scripture which justified their methods. Cox does not have this going for him. His doctrine of Scripture is as difficult to pick up as are his principles of hermeneutics, and I fancy something drastic is going to have to be done about both these matters before we can hope to make the Bible speak adequately and truly to our generation.

There are many other ways in which the unsatisfactory

character of Cox's *Scriptura ex machina* methodology could be illustrated. I will add only a few comments about the remarkable selectivity which he employs when it comes to providing himself with a biblical foundation for his ideas. Much use is made, for example, of the "prophetic" element in the Old Testament. But the whole of the more or less equally large "priestly" tradition is rather conveniently left out of consideration. And even in the prophetic material, only such factors as are suitable to theses Dr. Cox is presenting are allowed to figure in the discussion. What, for instance, about the strongly antiurban, anticivilizational emphases that run through the pre-eighth-century prophetic strain and are to be found even in some of the great canonical prophets themselves? And if, as Cox maintains, the Exodus involves the desacralization of politics (pp. 25 ff.), why does the sacral kingship play so large a part in later Israelite history and why do the psalms associated with this view come to have an honored place in the worship of the Hebrew people? Medieval Christianity, with its sacral civilization, is accused of perpetrating a "fatal respatialization of Christianity" (p. 58), as though such a procedure involved an overt flight in the face of explicit biblical principles. But doesn't this sound rather like saying only that they were not fortunate enough to have had the sociological training of the modern age (and of Harvey Cox) to enable them to perceive the hidden subtleties of the Exodus story? It seems to me obvious that they were convinced they had plenty of Scriptural justification, especially in the Old Testament, for what they believed and argued, and on the surface I cannot see how it can be said that they did not. Cox chooses to stress some aspects of the Bible, while they found it advantageous to stress others, and it appears to me to be grossly anachronistic to accuse them of thereby transmuting the Gospel into a Baal cult. This kind of ahistorical labeling does not really get us far. How can we go about showing that, in spite of large parts of the Bible and its apparent repeated assertions to the contrary, the kind of reading that Cox feels can be reconciled with what is distinctive and valuable in modern secular life can be shown to be not only discernible in isolated sections of Scripture, but also fundamental to the genius of the Bible as a whole? Our author's biblical work, with its "catch-as-catch-can" variety of selectivity, is not really very helpful in this regard.

I have by no means exhausted all that could be said by way of criticism of the manner in which *The Secular City* appeals to Scripture, but space forbids my pursuing the point much further. I will make one final jab. I detect not only a tendency to a *Scriptura ex machina* type of exegesis in this book, but also a rather unfortunate habit of falling back on a *Doctor ex machina* kind of authoritarianism when the possibility exists that Cox's point might seem too far-fetched to be credible. On at least three occasions he offers us some highly speculative pieces of biblical interpretation and then proceeds to call to his assistance a scholar who rather coincidentally happens, on the basis of his scientific investigations, to have arrived at conclusions completely in accord with the position being maintained. The problem is that on each of these three occasions it seems quite clear that a wide variety of opinion is likely to be found among the experts with regard to just the matters under consideration. But no reference to this state of affairs is made at all. No word of caution is allowed to dull the impact of the author's confident invocation of his scholarly allies' names, even though an opposing viewpoint could just as plainly be presented with an equally imposing display of "big brass" support.

For example, after outlining von Rad's views on the theological significance of Genesis 2:4 ff., this remarkable passage occurs:

> Generations of biblical scholars, charmed by the spell of the Greeks, have overlooked or minimized the astonishing fact that creation is *not* completed by God in the Bible until after man is formed and begins to work as God's partner in ordering the chaos. This means, in effect, that creation is *never* really "complete." The Genesis stories depict something that man and God are always doing (p. 76).

Frankly, despite the sweeping assurance of the tone of this statement, I cannot see that it differs very much from saying simply, "I think von Rad is right and everyone who disagrees with him is wrong." And that is hardly a sufficient foundation for the far-reaching theological generalization which Cox then sees fit to erect upon von Rad's opinion.

The same sort of criticism applies, in my view, to the introduction of the judgment of Amos Wilder on the Kingdom of God in the teaching of Jesus (pp. 111 ff.), and that of van Peursen on the notion of *'emeth* as covenant dependability (p. 64 ff.). In all three cases the scholars are competent and significant, but their word does not settle the issue by any stretch of the imagination. To imply that it does come close to what the ancient logicians called *argumentum ad verecundiam,* and in the text books I studied, that was treated as an example of the fallacy of avoiding the point at issue. I do not say that Cox is consciously taking an easy way out. But his tendency to employ the pontifical pronouncement, buttressed by the view of some convenient and weighty scholarly mentor, is much too prone to create the impression that on *this* particular issue at any rate no further intelligent discussion is conceivable—when, as a matter of fact, in any number of cases throughout the book, nothing could be further from the truth.

This concluding point could perhaps be said to sum up the criticism I would offer of Cox's use of the Bible. And it could be applied to several other aspects of *The Secular City* as well. He makes it all sound far too simple. He does not take into account with anything like adequacy the vast differences between the world views of the biblical writers and the outlook of the modern secular society which he celebrates. Sometimes he seems almost to be inviting us to his own particular brand of "Back-to-the-Bible" crusade, so scornful is he of tradition and the past nineteen centuries of Christian history. It is hardly disputable that we must certainly go to the Bible if what we are to present to our generation is to be genuinely Christian. But it is doubtful whether the kind of biblicism Cox appears to opt for will be able to carry us through in the end. There are many more problems than he takes note of, or even hints at, and there is much more hard work ahead of us than he seems to imply.

Perhaps the book was written for an audience which could

not be expected to comprehend the intricacies of critical biblical and historical scholarship. In that case, some latitude will, of course, have to be allowed. But I wonder whether it is really the best thing to suggest to anybody today, and especially to those who cannot check it out for themselves, that the gap between the Bible and the twentieth century is not as wide as they might have been led to believe. It is wide, and there are no short-cuts around it. It can only be bridged by careful research and reflection. Slogans and oversimplifications will not help. *The Secular City* would be less liable to mislead if this had been made considerably more evident.

# CHAPTER 7

# Urban Renewal in the Holy City

## Ruel Tyson

If one assumes *The Secular City* to be a sign pointing to an analysis and description in sociological or historical modes, he will be misconstruing Professor Cox's announced intention. Cox's primary interest is not in actual cities, a utopian city, or exclusively in "urbanism as a way of life." The crucial phrase in the subtitle "in theological perspective" decisively qualifies both "urbanization" and "secularization." Within his theological perspective Cox is working in an economy of symbol management.

Properly transcribed "for our times," the secular city is a symbol of "the biblical image of the Kingdom of God" (p. 116). With urbanization included, "this brings to the symbol the enrichment of an impressive heritage of 'city' symbols from the New Jerusalem and the City of God to the New Creation as Metropolis . . ." (p. 109). If one follows Cox's direction, it is possible to understand the function of his discussion of secularization and urbanization. Consideration of such topics performs the work of symbol enrichment. Unless the book is viewed in this manner *The Secular City* needs extensive city planning. For Cox moves with amazing dexterity between general descriptions of present urban life to historical assertions and from both to predictive and normative judgments.

"Secularization arises in large measure from the formative influence of biblical faith on the world, an influence mediated first by the Christian church and later by movements deriving partly from it" (p. 21). Cox tells his readers that "secularization as a descriptive term has a wide and inclusive significance." This statement is immediately followed by a combined predictive and normative statement: "Secularization implies a historical process, almost certainly irreversible, in which society and culture are delivered from tutelage to religious control and closed metaphysical world views. We have argued that it is basically a liberating development" (p. 20).

If the work were primarily historical there would be urgent reasons to enter the lists with Cox on the question of what constitutes "a historical movement." He says that "secularization" is a historical movement and "secularism" is an ideology. "The two should never be confused. Secularization is a liberating process. . . . Secularism short-circuits the secular revolution by freezing it into a new world view" (p. 86; *cf.* pp. 18–21). Presumably, ideologies are not distinctive elements in historical movements. No one would wish to be charged with blacking-out the secular revolution through ideological short-circuiting; but behind the slippery term "ideology" stands a well-placed question: What status is accorded to thought in historical causality and influence? Within such stringent definitions how would the thought of Copernicus and Kant be judged? Are they "secularists" or "secularizers"? If they are secularizers, is their thought to be accounted for by showing the formative influence of biblical faith on their persons and work?

Sometimes Cox understands a man's thought by claiming it is a manifestation of a certain cultural mood, as in the case of his discussion of Paul Tillich (pp. 79–81). Sometimes Cox explains intellectual systems by claiming they betray certain psychological needs in their creators as well as bearing the mark of "unbelief," as in the case of his remarks about "the ontologist" (p. 66). At other times he does not pursue one of the varieties of reductionism which recur throughout his book, as in the case of his discussion of Karl Barth (pp. 82–84).

"When man changes his tools and his techniques, his ways of producing and distributing the goods of life, he also changes his gods. Tribal, town, and technopolitan existence represent first of all different forms of social, economic, and political community. As such they symbolize different religions or belief systems" (p. 8). Here there is a clear declaration about priority in the determination of religious or belief systems. In other places in his work, Cox accepts a modified psychoanalytical mode of explanation, using the concepts of sublimation and projection (p. 150). His position on historical relativism, which he says is the "end product of secularization," is unclear (pp.32–34). In its irrepressible ubiquity "the secularization process" is presumably only relative in its local expressions.

Using a set of distinctions alien to Cox's own, the secularity of *The Secular City* is to be found in the tacit and often contradictory categorial commitments Cox employs, particularly with regard to methods of explanation and assessment of thought, value, and symbol. However, the important issue is elsewhere.

Has Cox committed himself to modes of explanation which, if applied to his own basic norm, the Bible, systematically erode that norm and consequently the ground of the entire argument? Does Cox want to account for "changes" in biblical history—Exodus (pp. 25 ff.) and Sinai (pp. 30 ff.), for example—by claiming there were previous changes in "tools," "techniques," and "ways of producing and distributing the goods of life"? He writes at length about "the relativization of values" (pp. 31–36). "Like nature and politics, they [values] are no longer the direct expression of the divine will. They have become what certain people at a particular time and place hold to be good. ("After all, it is God—not the Girl—who is God. He is the center and source of value" [p. 199; *cf.* p. 215].) They have ceased to be values and have become valuations" (p. 31). Does Cox want to say that the "valuations" he makes about interdependence, responsible freedom, maturity, openness have no status but in opinion or consensus? That they are not backed by "the biblical view"? And, if these valuations are backed by "the biblical view," how is access to this view possible in the secular cities of the present, "a new situation which renders former ways of thinking and doing wholly obsolete" (p. 117)?

However these questions are answered, they refer to confusions in methodology and language and are not central to

Cox's own interests. These citations, and the questions they elicit, are helpful in allowing the reader to discover how the term "secularization" is being used in this theological discourse. Secularization refers to the "content of man's coming of age" (p. 4). It is a "liberating process"; it makes possible and demands "maturity." Much of the discussion of secularization, therefore, is a means for elaborating a normative character type. The emergent "technopolitan" as portrayed by Cox continues a form of study made famous by those quaint townsmen Aristotle and Theophrastus and pursued today quite differently in the respected work of Erik Erikson. While he writes at some length about urbanization as the content of this new man, Cox is more concerned with a normative characterology than he is with descriptive studies of actual men and women in cities of advanced industrial societies.* Predicates like "mature," "responsible," "open," and "pragmatic" indicate the "style" of this new man. In other times and places they would be called "the virtues."

In spite of the elusive mixture of different types of statements in the book there is an overriding order to be found. There are two schemata which inform most of the many parts of the work. These frameworks constitute the author's argument; they structure the program of theological assimilation; and they manage, not without severe strain, his use of descriptive material.

Faced with an exploding metropolis, Cox offers a program of urban renewal which appeals to the biblical sources of secularization. A central proposal is that the biblical sources

* One has to exercise extreme caution in deciding the status of statements made about "technopolitan man" or the "secular city." Does this type of man in this new setting now exist? The author says that the new character and his new context are in process of development: "Technopolis represents a new species of human community. The fact that it is a neologism will remind us that it is not yet achieved in reality. . . . We are all tribal, town, and technopolitan to some degree, but technopolitan culture is the wave of the future" (p. 6). The secularization process is "almost certainly irreversible" (p. 20). Yet there are powers in the secular city that "represent the constant danger of relapsing into tribal thralldom which haunts the secular society . . ." (p. 204). There is "the lure of town culture, the period we have most recently left behind, at least in most respects" (p. 205).

of secularization must be uncovered once more "to strengthen our capacity to deal with secularization today by showing where it came from" (p. 17). Even though it is asserted that the present shape and style of the secular city is due in large measure to the influence of biblical faith, it is still necessary to uncover this momentous fact again. Moreover, such un-covering will "strengthen our capacity to deal with secularization." Yet "secularization itself can be viewed as a process of maturing and assuming responsibility" (p. 119).

To understand the present and to gain sustenance for life in the present Cox proposes a return to the true origins of the present. To find out what they are now, secular men must discover anew how they began; to discover present identity they must return to their origins. Their true origins reside in the "biblical version," "the biblical view," or the Bible.

The recurrent theme is that of return to origins (pp. 17, 65, 113, 204). This is not a difficult task, for it turns out that secular, profane, pragmatic, relativistic, functional, anony-mous, and mobile men of the present correspond to or can be reconciled with biblical understandings of profanity, truth, value, politics, nature, and mobile forms of life—all of which were and are typical of men of biblical faith.

The proposal is *regressus ad originem* which uncovers astounding congruities between the present style and shape of secular men and their counterparts in biblical history. In spite of the negative judgments Cox makes about "religion," such a proposal, the recollection of archaic realities or pri-mordial origins, is a classic religious strategy.* The conserva-tive and salutary function of memory is to recover true iden-tity, or to use Cox's favorite term, to achieve "maturity." The exemplary story which discloses the true biography of secular men is written in the Bible.

If return to origins is a decisive motif in *The Secular City,* the rejection of repressive supports from the past is equally important, especially "religious and metaphysical supports":

---

* See the discussion of Mircea Eliade, *Myths, Dreams and Mysteries: the encounter between contemporary faiths and archaic realities,* translated by Philip Mairet (London: Harvill Press, 1960), pp. 47–56. Cox points out that historians of religion illuminate cultural behavior "by studying it in the perspectives of the mythologies of bygone ages" (pp. 193–194).

But religion, instead of freeing man to play his part in the
making of the secular city, has frequently served as precisely that vehicle which has kept him in bondage to his
past, which has tied him to the childhood of the species.
. . . The maturation process in cultures and in individuals
is analogous. Consequently, the cultural equivalent of
infantile regression and childhood fears and fantasies can
be found in the religion of a given culture. Religion is, in
a sense, the neurosis of cultures; secularization corresponds
to maturation (pp. 152–153).

This type of psychogenetic schema frequently informs Cox's
exposition (*cf.* pp. 34, 109, 119–121, 150–153, 158–159). In
this framework personal and communal archaic heritages are
the opposites of secularization and maturation; the backward
look prevents "liberation" and maturity.

The logics of origin and continuity on which Cox depends
for much of his discussion of secularization  do not serve him
well when he sets forth the virtues of the normative character, the "unreligious" secular man. In the discussion of inde-
pendence, maturity, of "man come of age," the necessity for
liberation from the venerable tutors of memory, myth, and
tradition become paramount. On the one hand, identity is
procured by the uncovering of authentic origins; on the other,
maturity requires autonomy from such archaic forms, values,
and meanings. Cox brings the two schemata together:

> These images of maturity and responsibility are crucial
> for our argument here since secularization itself can be
> viewed as a process of maturing and assuming responsi-
> bility. Secularization signifies the removal of religious and
> metaphysical supports and putting man on his own. It
> is opening the door of the playpen and turning man loose
> in an open universe. Consequently it is important to notice
> that maturation and responsibility symbols are in no sense
> exceptional in the New Testament (p. 119).

While writing about secularization as a process in western
history, Cox refers to the origin of this process and to its
almost irreversible thrust. While sketching the portrait of the
fully secular man, Cox says that this man must be free from
tutelage to authority, particularly the enslaving authority of

the past; from infancy and adolescence in personal history; from tribe and town in communal history. For Cox there is no contradiction here, since secularization as a historical process defines the present social context and makes possible the emergence of technopolitan man. This interpretation of history is intended to support as well as elicit this new man. There is congruity between character and social structure, at least in imminent prospect if not in present fact.

However, Cox places some important qualifications on this crucial point in the second half of the book. For it appears that there is not only a heavy residue of tribalism in the secular city; there are also demonic forces, or despotic powers which "represent the constant danger of relapsing into tribal thralldom" (p. 204). This danger not only haunts the secular city; this statement and others like it (pp. 192, 205) haunt the earlier prediction that the process of secularization "is almost certainly irreversible" (p. 20).

The place of religion in the two frameworks employed by Cox is manifestly unclear. Early in the book the following statements are made: "The gods of traditional religions live on as private fetishes or the patrons of congenial groups, but they play no role whatever in the public life of the secular metropolis" (p. 2). "The age of the secular city . . . *is* an age of 'no religion at all' " (p. 3). This theme is continued later:

> The world is becoming more and more "mere world." It is being divested of its sacral and religious character. Man is becoming more and more "man" and losing the mythical meanings and cultic after-glows that marked him during the "religious" stage of history, a stage now coming to its end. Man must now assume the responsibility for his world. He can no longer shove it off on some religious power (p. 217).

In other places the theme and the focus change. Modern, secular man does experience the transcendent, "that which is not part of the self's equipment but comes beyond the self. No doubt urban-secular man experiences the transcendent in a radically different *way* than did his tribal and town forebears" (pp. 260–261). Does this new experience of the transcendent make secular man nonreligious *or* religious in novel ways?

Religious behavior is not absent in the epoch of technopolis. "Even in the emerging secular city, massive residues of magical and superstitious world views remain" (p. 150). And Cox laments the "continuing incapacity of theological critics to recognize the religious significance of cultural phenomena outside the formal religious system itself" (p. 198).

In *The Secular City* the reader is told of "unexorcised demons"; of the "church as cultural exorcist"; and of "the *mysterium tremendum* of the sexual." If the reader is given assertion about the absence of religion in one place, he is offered numerous references to its presence in another; frequently the author's rhetoric reminds him of the presence of that ghost.

Again, Cox's schema, which stresses continuity of the secularization process, its direction toward the goal of final secularity, is strained by his perception of the religious residue and of new forms of religious experience in contemporary culture. The schema thus structured cannot allow for resacralization as well as for secularization. Often his descriptions of contemporary life require a dialectical movement between the secular and the sacral processes; it is this dialectic that his goal-oriented, linear schema cannot provide.

No matter what precise, or imprecise, relations obtain between "secular" and "religious," both terms are not being employed in the interests of cultural diagnosis, the analysis of behavior, or description of actual men in their multiple forms of living. Both terms are dedicated to the enrichment of traditional Christian symbols, like "city," and traditional Christian virtues, like "sonship" and "stewardship."

It would be a mistake to assume that Cox has addressed his book to people who do not qualify for membership in *The Secular City*. Cox is quite definite with regard to his readers: "Clearly, those whose present orientation to reality is shaped by the biblical faith can hardly in good faith enter the lists as adversaries of secularization. Our task should be to nourish the secularization process, to prevent it from hardening into a rigid world view, and to clarify as often as necessary its roots in the Bible" (p. 36). Surely there are secular men who are not necessarily secularists whose orientations to reality are not shaped by biblical faith.

The singular merit of his book is that it presents in a rhetoric of relevance strong support for those whose orientation is shaped by biblical faith. Within the economy of Cox's theological perspective, participation in the urban world is legitimated for Christian folk. The received symbols are re-affirmed for those who accredit them as efficacious, and they are renewed by theological definitions of the secular:

> Christians believe God is at work in history bringing man to adulthood and responsibility. Within this framework the norms by which we make our decisions are fashioned and discarded in a continuing conversation with the Bible and with the culture, a conversation that is never completed. The Christian knows he is free only as a partner in this conversation and as a member of this community (p. 215).

Harvey Cox has given his readers a composite of the secular city in sacred perspective. In order that the other part of the conversation be initiated his readers may hope that he will not delay in presenting the sacred city in secular perspective.

A refined description of the present and appreciative understanding of its elusively disjunctive values and meanings does not yet appear to be one of the preoccupations of theologians. There may be ample reason for this crucial poverty in much current theological writing. A full reading of the form and spirit of modern theology in its own terms could destroy the assumption of relevance which is pervasive in theologies of correlation or of assimilation. Such destruction may be unthinkable, though it could provide the occasion for considering the virtues of irrelevance, especially ways of gaining critical distance on present social and cultural configurations.

Instead of joining forthrightly in "the tradition of the new," with its irony, foolishness, and risk, strategists of theological assimilation assume the current availability of traditions of the old. Older forms of order and meaning are assumed to have capacities to encompass in some manner the present. The summary assumption is that revolution can be understood and criticized by reappropriating the riches of the traditional regime; there is nothing new under the sons of the father—even when sons, in images of revolt, declare themselves bastards. Assimilation or adoption can legitimate the most imperious impiety.

# PART TWO

# The *Christianity and Crisis* Debate

# CHAPTER 1

# What It Means to Be Secular

## *Charles C. West*

What does it mean to be secular in the modern urban world? Harvey Cox's book *The Secular City* contains two levels of answer which reflect the bifurcation of the whole current debate.

In one obvious and demonstrable way modern city and industrial life has become functional, mobile, organizational and political as distinct from that which is communal, stable and imbued with cultural values and controls. Everything has its function to perform and its time to last. This, rather than its status as part of a timeless order of society and nature, defines its being.

But in a deeper sense, to be secular is to take this social inevitability into one's own soul and to be confronted thereby with the question whether and in what way one can speak in a secular fashion of God. This is the burden of Cox's final chapter. It is also the key to the whole problem with which he deals.

The concept "God" has become problematic for modern secular man in a different way from that shown by Bertrand Russell, Julian Huxley and the scientific humanists of a past generation. The "death of God" thinkers in our time are a diverse fraternity, but they have one common belief. They are not simple atheists or agnostics, complacent in their rationalist structures and methods, but men who have made a decision about events and powers in history and about man's calling and destiny. "If God did exist, it would be necessary to abolish Him," Cox paraphrases the conviction of Albert Camus.

Nietzsche, Marx, the Russian atheists of the nineteenth century and the modern existentialists all recognize, however indirectly, that there has been a power in the world that went by the name of God. He was once a force to be reckoned with, if only as the objective embodiment of a dehumanized class existence (Marx), of servile morality (Nietzsche) or of the tyrannical order for whose sake men are condemned to suffer (Belinsky and Ivan Karamazov).

Once "God" organized man's world and controlled his history; He does so no more. Other powers have taken over; "God" is dead. Dietrich Bonhoeffer and Cox give their theological support to this conviction.

The God who was a working hypothesis for explaining and excusing the way of the world, the Zeus of the Greeks, the Unmoved Mover of Aristotle, the God of the theistic philosophers and of conservative social order has indeed been crowded to the edge of the world. The world is becoming increasingly nonreligious, if "religion" is defined as the need for such an eternal order or ruler. Honest thought and responsible action require that we no longer reckon with this "God."

What then takes the place of God? What are the dimensions of secular existence? Here the spirits divide. For Nietzsche, Marx and Belinsky, it is man who must become sovereign, man as "free, creative self-activity" (Marx) organizing and using power to subdue nature and express his freedom. It is Superman who must emerge from the struggle, discipline and work that this involves.

"I love those," wrote Nietzsche, "who do not first seek a reason beyond the stars for going down and being sacrifices, but sacrifice themselves to the earth, that the earth of the Superman may hereafter live." No Marxist, no research technologist in a DuPont laboratory could have put it better.

Harvey Cox gives full place to this faith and motivation. There is just a wee bit of Nietzsche in him. He does not, of course, replace God with man. He speaks with conviction about the "One we meet both in the life of Jesus and in our present history as the liberator and the hidden one." But he draws out of the Bible primarily the relation of partnership between man and God in organizing the world.

It is the function of all things that counts as we determine it pragmatically. The truth is not over against man, but man *does* it as he handles power responsibly. The relation of the team and the working group replaces the community. The discipline and renunciation that such creative work requires is repentance, and the responsibility resulting therefrom serves the Kingdom of God.

This view has its biblical roots. It is the meaning of that abused word "stewardship," especially as Paul uses it to speak of his "stewardship of God's grace" that is the "plan of the mystery hidden for ages in God who created all things" (Ephesians 3:2, 9). It is a restatement of the truth that the Social Gospel contained in terms of a theology of God's reconciling power over the structures and powers of modern society. *In* his free, creative, responsible work man discovers what is means to be related to God, who is also at work and calls man to be his partner.

Secular existence has another side, however. Not always can the man who has experienced the death of God be quite so sure that there is hope in man. Camus for one was far from sure. "God is denied in the name of justice," he wrote, "but can the idea of justice be understood without the idea of God?" Man, who defies God for his tyranny, puts his own standards and values in God's place. The justified rebellion becomes an ideology of revolution, and man becomes the victim of a new tyranny set up by his own ideal. The only answer, as Camus sees it, is always to be a rebel, to fight for and discover such humanity as we discover case by case but never to surrender to the illusions of hope, be it theistic or humanist.

But can man do this, given the kind of a being he knows himself to be? His problem is the unavoidable guilt that his relations with his fellow men involve. "Once secularized," Gabriel Vahanian writes with Franz Kafka in mind but quoting Camus, "innocence defeats itself, whereas in the strange solidarity of guilt from which no one is excluded, much less by putting on the mask of innocence, 'every man testifies to the crime of all.' "

The pathos of this situation is that there is no God to excuse or cover over; for just this reason the guilt is both the substance of human existence and its destruction. This also is the drama of the secular city. It helps explain why so many people there drift and die.

This side of secularity too has its biblical foundations. The forgiveness of God and the new life in Christ that is possible in the face of guilt have nothing to do with the excusing of man's inhumanity to man. It is life in which the death of self is a daily experience as well as an accomplished fact. It is life prepared not only to function, to manage and to organize, but to wait, to listen, to serve where others are directing and to suffer. It is life whose essence is still confrontation with an Other who judges (perhaps in the form of what the victims of our prosperity think of us) and creates from His side a new relationship, in which work in partnership may then be possible.

The great weakness of *The Secular City* is that it says so little about all this. The book will be welcomed by multitudes of Americans for what it is not intended to be—a return to the robust liberalism of the days before Reinhold Niebuhr, the Great Depression and the Communist challenge—with God lined up to help achieve the best-intended plans of men. It will undergird the good conscience, and thereby the insensitivity and pride, of technicians, managers, statesmen and revolutionaries who are "doing all they can" within the limits of their own security, interests and control to solve the problems of society.

In short, it neglects the margin that exists between the highest achievements of human goodness and the minimum necessary to bring health and peace to the world—the margin expressed in the Bible by the crucifixion of Christ.

At one point the author claims that "we are trying to live in a period of revolution without a theology of revolution." The fact is that the generation just past produced the finest crop of theologies for revolution that Christian history has ever seen, beginning with Nicholai Berdyaev, continuing in a different way with Karl Barth, the Reinhold Niebuhr of the 1930s, Josef Hromadka and the Dietrich Bonhoeffer of the *Letters and Papers from Prison*. These men were all profounder, however, than the present book, because they under-

stood the dilemma of the strong and free man whose very
strength is his problem when he seeks to restore and deepen
the relations with his fellow men and with God that he himself has broken.

There are times in the life of the secular city and in the
course of a revolution when one is called not to be active but
passive, not to talk but to listen, not to organize but to suffer
the mismanagement of others, or their misunderstanding,
scorn or hatred, if not their more violent attacks. There are
times when one is called to live with insoluble problems without the illusion that some politics or technology can get rid of
them. From the hydrogen bomb to the narcotics addict—
these are our daily responsibility.

In the Old Testament it was the suffering servant who
faithfully brought forth justice (Isaiah 42:3). Cox is right
that the secular city is a place of hope where the living God
of biblical history can be discovered and believed. What a
shame that his book leaves out the dimension of human relations broken and remade by the forgiveness and grace by
which all of us live, which gives this believing secularity its
mystery and depth.

# CHAPTER 2

# Chalcedon in Technopolis

## Paul Lehmann

It is not often one reads a book that both changes one's mind and alters one's habits of thought. Harvey Cox's *The Secular City* has done this both *for* me and *to* me. I can, therefore, best underline its importance and celebrate its appearance by trying to describe the sense in which these changes have occurred.

Naturally such an attempt includes the hope that the book will receive the widest possible attention and produce similar results for others who read it. But whether it does or not, the significance of the book is undiminished.

In a style at once crisp, concrete, and vivid, by means of an analysis that is both sound and original, and in passages of unusual brilliance, Dr. Cox has brought theological and sociological findings and insights together in an impressive description of the creative connection between Christian orthodoxy and the industrial, urban society that "shapes our ends, rough-hew them how we will."

The symbol of this connection from the side of Christian orthodoxy is Chalcedon, from the side of urban industrialism, technopolis. According to Cox, technopolis is unintelligible apart from Chalcedon; Chalcedon, far from being a relic of a dead and distant past, is the center and sense of what is going on in technopolis. In short, Chalcedon has come to technopolis. And Christians are once again, as they have been before, equipped to know the score.

Of course, some will regard this estimate of what Cox has put before us as extravagant. They may be correct. But let them not too quickly celebrate the wisdom of their own con-

ceit without a careful pause over the possibility that they may
have concluded too quickly that they have known it all already.

Perhaps the crucial passage in the book is also the one that
underlies this assessment of its significance. It may, therefore,
not be improper to quote at some length from it.

> Is Jesus God or man? Does his life represent an act of
> God for man or the full response of a man to God? The
> perennial answer of theologians has always been that He
> is both, and that the amounts of one or the other are not
> measurable. When the problem was discussed in the
> language of Greek substance philosophy, the formulation
> of the Council of Chalcedon held that Jesus was fully God
> *and* fully man. When the same discussion is translated into
> the vocabulary of contemporary social change, the issue
> is whether history, and particularly revolution, is some-
> thing that happens *to* man or something that man *does*.
> Social determinists have battled with advocates of some-
> thing called the "freedom of the individual" over this ques-
> tion for years. Is man the subject or the object of social
> change?
>
> The only convincing answer is that he is both, and efforts
> to sort out amounts of one or the other inevitably fail.
> True, there are moments when man seems to step out and
> launch vast new initiatives. There are other periods when
> the tides of history seem to sweep man along despite all
> he can do. But the secular city, the fusion of secularization
> and urbanization, stands for that point where social move-
> ment and human initiative intersect, where man is free
> not in spite of but because of the social matrix in which
> he lives. Just as some theologians have interpreted the
> deity of Jesus as his readiness to accept and execute God's
> purpose for him, so the secular city signifies that point
> where man takes responsibility for directing the tumultuous
> tendencies of his time.
>
> The Kingdom of God, concentrated in the life of Jesus
> of Nazareth, remains the fullest possible disclosure of the
> partnership of God and man in history. Our struggle for
> the shaping of the secular city represents the way we
> respond faithfully to this reality in our own times (pp.
> 111–112).

Here we have the insights and language of theological orthodoxy translated by the language of social change. Conversely, the insights and language of social change are illumined by the insights of theological orthodoxy. Here concerns and concepts that have marked the theological tumult of this century are carried beyond the polarities that used to set dogma against life, theology against culture, the Bible against history, Church against world, God against man.

Here concerns and concepts that have marked the sociological tumult of this century are carried beyond the stereotypes that have paralyzed the possibility of a creative correlation of objective and subjective factors in human nature, of ideational and behavioral aspects of human relations, judgments, and decisions, of determinism and freedom, of direction and responsibility in the dynamics of social change. Above all, here the matrix within which and by which what man thinks and does is being concretely shaped intersects the matrix within which and by which what man thinks and does acquires meaning, destiny, purpose.

It is this intersection that best explains the sense in which this book has changed my mind. What Cox's account of the secular city has done *for* me is to set the major ambiguities of life in technopolis in a positive framework of freedom and responsibility. Anonymity, mobility, bureaucracy, and organization—which I had hitherto regarded as the principal foci of dehumanization in modern society—I have now come to see as the principal foci at which the purpose and activity of God and the responsibility and activity of man for the humanization of man in society intersect.

It had always seemed to me that mobility and organization were unavoidable, if sometimes regrettable, facts of life in a world shaped by movement and machines. Anonymity and bureaucracy, however, had always seemed to me fundamentally expendable. I thought it all but impossible that these features of technopolis could be instrumental to any constructive human and social purpose. Now I see these features the other way. They still exhibit ambiguity; that is, they are not without actual and potential corruption. But they are intrinsically positive rather than negative because they serve the concrete function of furthering rather than obstructing humanization.

As Cox has put it:

> From this perspective, urbanization can be seen as a liberation from some of the cloying bondages of preurban society. It is the chance to be free. Urban man's . . . being anonymous to most people permits him to have a face and a name for others. . . . The sore point is *not* that these massive bureaucratic empires exist. The problem is that we have not yet learned how to control them for the common welfare (pp. 47, 174).

I am not a little grateful to Cox for a simple but wonderful thing: the refusal to answer the telephone no longer need be an occasion of guilt.

The reading of *The Secular City* has also done something *to* me. It has altered my way of approaching theology. Involved here is not so much a reversal of viewpoint as a shift of accent: my interpretation of Christian doctrine has lost its self-containment. The inner logic of Christian theology is no longer an account of the inner cogency of any given rational pattern or structure of thought. It has become instead an analysis of the function of theological ideas as conceptual symbols that express the images, memories, experiences of a particular segment of mankind on the journey from Exodus to Easter. This journey intersects with the pilgrimage of all mankind from tribe to technopolis.

The language of such a functional theology refines and amplifies its meaning primarily neither by metaphysical borrowings nor by language games, but by the relations and functions, the signs and symbols that are the "stuff" of man's concrete social behavior and development. Cox states it this way:

> The grammar of the Gospel is not a categorical imperative; it first of all points to what *is* occurring, only secondarily does it call for a consequent change in attitude and action. The Kingdom of God is at hand; therefore repent. The syntax of the secular city is identical. Through its

irrepressible emergence it establishes a new situation which renders former ways of thinking and doing wholly obsolete. . . . It creates its own gap, catalyzing man to close it if he wishes to remain man and not be overwhelmed by the forces of history (pp. 116–117).

The title of the book is a conspicuous example of its major significance. It might have been called *Preface to a Revolutionary Theology*, but the title it actually bears is a vivid sign of a functional theology in action.

That such a venture should be marked by debatable points of view or even by exaggerations is to be expected. But let those who are tempted to exaggerate the exaggerations or to minimize the principal thrust of *The Secular City*, or both, take care lest they deliver theological and sociological analysis over to the desultory business of straining at gnats and swallowing camels.

In 1932 Reinhold Niebuhr broke fresh ground for Christian faith and thought by crossing over from theology and ethics into politics. *Moral Man and Immoral Society* became a landmark in the theological and sociological analysis of power. Of the phenomenon of power Cox's book takes insufficient account. Nonetheless, it is in its own way a not dissimilar landmark in theological and sociological analysis. This time the accent is upon the dynamics, the constructive possibilities and responsibilities for social change. It should be read and pondered with the utmost seriousness.

# CHAPTER 3

# The Social Gospel Revisited

## *David Little*

In reading the recent religious literature on "secularization," particularly Harvey Cox's *The Secular City*, one gets the impression that he has heard this song before. The tempo is different; some of the lyrics have changed. But the melody, unpopular for so long it was nearly forgotten, is unmistakable. Here is a tune composed and made famous well over fifty years ago by the Social Gospel movement. The reader is, therefore, astonished by claims that *The Secular City* is a profound breakthrough, something brand new.

What is really startling about the book is the response it has received. When the Social Gospel tune was played in the thirties, forties and fifties, it was met with disdain and condescension. Now, in the 1960s—by means of Cox's artful rendition—it is suddenly (once again) a "hit."

In 1917 Walter Rauschenbusch wrote:

> The Kingdom ideal contains the revolutionary force of Christianity. . . . It translates theology from the static to the dynamic. . . . The Kingdom of God, at every stage of human development, tends toward a social order which will best guarantee to all personalities their freest and highest development. . . . [It] is not a concept nor an ideal merely, but an historical force. It is a vital and organizing energy now at work in humanity.

Soon after Rauschenbusch produced these words, a generation of theologians rose up in consternation. Such simpleminded progressivism had nothing to do with the Christian faith!

Almost fifty years later Cox, with ostensible originality, informs us that we need a "theology of social change," of revolution. The keystone of his "new theology" is, interestingly enough, the Kingdom of God. The Kingdom for him is interrelated, if not identical, with the worldwide process of secularization, which is "a process of maturing and assuming responsibility." In it "God is ever at work making freedom and personhood possible." Cox says:

> The biblical image of the Kingdom of God, transcribed for our times into the symbol of the secular city, the commonwealth of maturity and interdependence, provides a catalytic gap. . . . Motion from here to there and from now to then fixes the crucial axis of the Bible. The Kingdom of God has never come in its fullness and perfection. . . . [It] is always just arriving (p. 116).

Cox writes these words and all trace of consternation, disdain and condescension is gone.

Rauschenbusch was considered unsophisticated and a shallow activist when he averred that "the Social Gospel is above all things practical," that it is secular in orientation, that "it is not primarily interested in metaphysical questions." Theologians were appalled by his "immanentalism," by his failure to appreciate the radical Otherness of God, when he pleaded for a God "immanent in humanity," one who "always urges the race on toward a higher combination of freedom and solidarity." They were very nearly apoplectic when he called God man's "chief fellow-worker."

But Cox uses almost identical language and people find him exciting. Metaphysical thought for Cox, as for Rauschenbusch, is through—it is a childish fascination that tends to impede rather than "urge on" what Cox calls the secularization process and Rauschenbusch called the social movement. We must use "secular" political language to talk about God. Accordingly, "We speak to [our neighbor] of God whenever we cause him to realize consciously the web of interhuman reciprocity." (Rauschenbusch's word for the same thing was "solidarism.")

Furthermore, Cox enjoins us to explore "the notions of

teamwork and partnership . . . in our conceptualization of God." "Like his relationship to his work partner, man's relationship to God derives from the work they do together." For Cox, man and God are none other than "fellow workers."

Finally, mature modern man is eminently pragmatic. He is concerned with practical social matters and is not, like Nazis and other "technological utopians," "bogged down in the metaphysical and religious stages of human development."

Our little comparison could be extended indefinitely, but the point is this: theology is a fickle business and, therefore, is subject to several disabilities. When books like *The Secular City* are written without the slightest acknowledgment or apparent awareness of the solid historical tradition in which they stand, and when they are similarly received, theological and ethical discussion is not advanced very far. The reason is that the hard, persistent problems raised by the tradition are overlooked or suppressed below the level of consciousness. Anyone who wishes to resuscitate the Social Gospel or something like it will need to deal more systematically and carefully with these problems than has been done so far.

To begin with, the acknowledgment of which I speak is only historical courtesy. Walter Rauschenbusch and company have been the objects of such scorn that those who once again wish to couch the Christian Gospel in the language of practical worldliness, of social revolution and development, might have the good form to pay their due respects. While by no means everything in *The Secular City* was said or even implied before, enough of it was that the similarities and parallels ought to be made explicit.

Moreover, such acknowledgment would extend some much-deserved credit to the Christian tradition. It is very misleading to object, as Cox does, that traditional Christian doctrines "are almost entirely past-oriented." Not only is the substance of Cox's own point of view quite "traditional," but the Social Gospel itself inherited a rich legacy of "constructive Protestantism," as H. Richard Niebuhr demonstrated so brilliantly in *The Kingdom of God in America*.

However, the hard problems remain. It is my impression that the collision of the Social Gospel with neoorthodoxy

earlier in this century sharpened several critical issues for the
Christian church that we still have on our hands. *The Secular
City* raises a number of these. We can deal with only one: the
problem of ethical and social theory.

The Social Gospel was not afraid to speak of and to utilize
values and principles in its social and ethical thinking. It
attempted to derive from doctrinal assumptions normative
institutional patterns such as "democracy" and "socialism,"
as well as specific social values such as "freedom," "solidarism" and "justice." In short, the Social Gospel tried (how
adequately is another question) to move back and forth between theological belief and ethical principle with some
semblance of method. For this the movement was roundly
criticized. Various brands of contextualism and situational-
ism, among other things, have violently protested over the
last thirty years that the Social Gospel values themselves *became* the Gospel, ignoring the Christian faith that God's
judgment rested on all human institutions and values.

Probably there is something in both positions, but the
manner in which Cox combines them—as he does unwit-
tingly—is to me thoroughly unsatisfactory. On the one hand,
Cox writes as an avowed contextualist:

> Value systems, like states and civilizations, come and go
> . . . symbol systems, the constellations of meaning by which
> human life is given value and direction, are seen as projec-
> tions of a given society. . . . Christian ethics must be un-
> reservedly contextual (p. 35).

On the other hand, what is pushed out the front door
barges right in at the back. The secularization process, as Cox
describes it, is decidedly *not* subject to the whims and con-
tingencies of historical men. It is painted "unreservedly" (and
I think a little crudely) as an objective process that is grind-
ing away through its developmental stages—religious, metaphysical and functional. Furthermore, it is dripping with specific values like "maturity," "accountability," "responsibility,"
"freedom," "interdependence" and "pragmatism." So far as
one can tell these values are unqualifiedly good because they

are the very entailments of the Kingdom of God toward which all is moving. Indeed, "the kerygma itself is articulated" when men recognize and act upon these desirable characteristics of the secular city.

But what precisely is going on here? All kinds of values and principles of a quite unrelativistic sort are at work, but they are blithely employed under the guise of an unprincipled contextualism. Because the author is not aware of what he is doing, his alleged contextualism in no way systematically qualifies the principles and values he affirms, but simply blinds him and the reader to the fact that he has been working with invariant values all along. Consequently, Cox exempts himself from the kind of precise ethical reflection that is required now as a result of the tensions between the Social Gospel and its critics.

What, in other words, is the status of values and norms in Christian ethics? Where exactly do we get them? In what specific ways should we employ them in decision-making? What is the relation of value to social development? To pose context over against principle, Gospel against Law simply does not help.

*The Secular City* raises other serious issues that we have no space to treat in detail. For one, we shall surely need a more refined understanding of "religion" in relation to society than Cox supplies. While social evolution is much under discussion these days, I know of no reputable sociologist who would think of introducing categories taken over from Auguste Comte to describe the process (Comte's stages of evolution were "primitive theological," "transient metaphysical" and "final positive").

Moreover, there is no careful treatment of what is meant by "religion," so that the notion of "religionless Christianity" is little more than a battle cry. I am not convinced that the term really makes any sense.

One is also disturbed by Cox's evaluation of the church in relation to society. He never explains, for example, why bureaucracies are virtually all good in the world and all bad in the church; why one is to promote rational bureaucratic action in the secular city, but sabotage it in the church. (He seems completely to miss one of Paul Harrison's central points in *Authority and Power in a Free Church Tradition*, that church bureaucracies serve very desirable, indeed indispensable, purposes.)

In summary, all those concerned to reconsider sympathetically, if objectively, the rich tradition of constructive Protestantism will be heartened by at least one thing Cox's book demonstrates: the latent virility of "the Kingdom of God in America." It is a good tradition, and in many ways it is very pertinent to our life and times. We can be grateful that Harvey Cox has—however unconsciously—revivified for us some of its themes and motifs in such an attractive way. But, alas, I seriously doubt that we shall serve either our heritage or ourselves very well if we continue to ignore that it *is* a tradition.

# CHAPTER 4

# Where Is the Church?

## C. Kilmer Myers

Harvey Cox has brought together in *The Secular City* many of the thoughts and feelings close to the church's level of consciousness as it prepares to live in the technopolitan age. He has even gently laid to rest many of the theological giants who, while they helped lead us to where we are, nonetheless worried us by their continued presence.

It is true that he is a bit glib, that he finishes off "systems" with rather neat dispatch. This may cause a certain uneasiness, but the punch is still present in what he writes.

Cox collates; he does not think originally, is no Richard Niebuhr agonizing over a problem in full view of the class. But he puts things together with skill, and we all ought to be grateful to him. He gives us a kind of textbook that summarizes our unspoken thoughts. He helps us move into a fantastically new day.

Harvey Cox moves me, which is to say that I think I "dig" him. He has written down what many of us in the Church talk about day and night albeit in bits and pieces. But I do not think he has a very exciting doctrine of the church, and it is about that alone that I offer a few disjointed comments.

Jesus is, he rightly says, the Kingdom. He is the Way. But Jesus is also the Church. I take this to be the statement of a radical ecclesiology. Jesus is Israel in his Person. The Body of Christ refers to his own body, not to a collection of persons. *He* is the People of God.

I would not dare to say that he is the substance of the church for fear of heresy in an ametaphysical age, so I will say that he somehow is the reality and the meaning of the

75

church. But Jesus is not the Head of a sect; he is the Head of Humanity. He *is* Man. The biblical view, as I understand it, is that he came into his own world *as* humanity. The church of God, therefore, is humanity. Or in the words of Father Gregory Baum, it is "the sacrament of Humanity."

Baptism, the rite of initiation into humanity, is birth. The Table of the Eucharist is the world itself. The bishop is the servant. A kind of amorphous mass now the church? It is the only doctrine of the church that makes sense in a secular age. Indeed the technological society now makes it possible to think in these terms. The "world" is a small room these days. The city makes possible communication, a new style of interpersonal relationships. God is revealing to us the reality of his church in social change.

If the church is, in the Pauline phrase, the Body of Christ, the basis for social decision rests upon the reality of this indissoluble union. The church is that which is, and, it would seem, we men require some sort of an IS if we are to function as men. The church, humanity, is the basis of all action because the church is Christ, the meaning of life and its end. That meaning and that end is making life more human—a responsibility given to us in the acts of creation. Each act of the church, however fractured by suburbanism, is a foretaste of things coming—the *time* when, in Augustine's words, there shall be one Christ loving himself.

I miss this in Cox and with it all the meaning of Catholicism.

# CHAPTER 5

# Does *The Secular City* Revisit the Social Gospel?

*George D. Younger*

David Little has made a peculiarly ahistorical appeal to history in his criticism of Harvey Cox's *The Secular City*. He accuses Cox of rehearsing the themes of the Social Gospel without giving due credit to their originals. By a selective comparison of quotes from Walter Rauschenbusch and *The Secular City*, he seeks to prove that both are guilty of "progressivism," "activism," "immanentalism," "solidarism," "pragmatism" and simple-minded reliance on partnership with God. His comparison does little justice either to Rauschenbusch or to Cox; it does even less to the almost sixty-year span that separates *Christianity and the Social Crisis* from *The Secular City*. If we are to appeal to history, let us not ignore what has happened in the meantime.

First, and probably most important, is the fact that a worldwide technological civilization has moved from possibility to actuality. Rauschenbusch was concerned about the implications of the possibility of tuberculin testing of cattle for a city's milk supply. Today we have the actuality of total control of human environment, whether in a Gemini capsule or an air-conditioned office building.

Dr. Little would have us believe that all this talk of "secularization" is only the old siren song of human progress that Western man has sung since the Renaissance. He neglects the evidence on every side that urban civilization, already made possible on every continent by the spread of technology, represents not a difference in degree from previous human societies but a difference in kind.

Technopolis is not the village and town with modern con-

veniences added; it is a new thing, not known to Augustine or
Aquinas, to Luther or Calvin, not even known to Rauschenbusch. No longer bound to gods of earth or society, no longer
tempted to serve other men as gods, man must accept his full
measure of responsibility for that which happens in this
world and must render true service to the sovereign God.

The most shattering result of the process of secularization
has been its denial of both privileged position and secure
sanctuary to the Christian church. The medieval assumption
that the church, through its knowledge of God, was necessarily in a position to know more and do more about the
world of nature and of men has been thoroughly exploded.
Now the church is freed to be servant, having been stripped
of its pretensions to majesty.

Also shattered has been the evangelical assumption that the
church, by dealing with men's private spiritual life, was doing
all that was needful. Now the church is called to the more
risky task of discerning the form of God's action and serving
Him in the common life of the world as well as within the
fellowship. Fastening God's name to the nation's flagpoles
and air-conditioning its sanctuaries, while seeming to hold
fast to the past, are actually fruits of secularism. Only a full
facing of the new situation into which Christians have been
thrust by secularization will produce acceptable fruits in the
church's life and theology.

Second, we must recognize that Cox's statement in *The
Secular City* is post-Barthian. One of the primary faults of
the Social Gospel was overreliance upon categories of immanence to describe God and His relation to men. This was a
failing its American exponents shared with the Continental
liberal theologians and Bible scholars from whom they se-
cured their intellectual undergarments. Seeing God principally in terms of His works in nature and the ethical fruits He
produced in the lives of men, they neglected that aspect of
biblical revelation which shows us God as *Pantocrator*, the
Almighty One who inhabits eternity.

The supreme contribution of the last generation in theology, especially of Karl Barth, has been the recovery of transcendence as the primary category under which to understand

and describe the God of the Bible. Barth's use of the razor
of revelation may at times have destroyed the possibility of
any legitimate relationship between transcendence and immanence in God's nature, but he quite thoroughly made his
point with the generation that has succeeded him: Unless
God be God, He cannot be God with us.

Cox is not engaging in intellectual gamesmanship when he
includes Barth's *Church Dogmatics* and *The Humanity of
God* in his bibliography. He already assumes the kind of
radical sovereignty for which Barth has spoken, even as did
Dietrich Bonhoeffer before him. The trouble is that he, like
Bonhoeffer, is understood both by critics and disciples to be
presenting an antithesis to the Barthian thesis. What we have
here is more like a post-Barthian synthesis that assumes much
of Barth's position while attempting to answer a different set
of questions in a different situation.

Third, we must also recognize that a generation of critics,
including Reinhold Niebuhr, has given the lie to the easy
optimism of the Social Gospel about the nature of social
change. Even in the more chastened statements of *A Theology for the Social Gospel* (1917), Walter Rauschenbusch
was still optimistic about the steady progress that men could
make in their life in society. But the very sentences Little
quotes as proof that Cox's book shares Rauschenbusch's
"simple-minded progressivism" are actually an indication that
he has listened to those who say it is never possible completely to equate that which men are doing with the fullness
and perfection of the Kingdom of God. Human sin and
temporal contingency guarantee that the secular city, while
bearing the marks of God's work, will never exhaust the
meaning of the Kingdom.

At times Cox's emphasis on the possibilities God has
placed within the secular city threatens to overwhelm his
appreciation of this fact. But it is not fair either to what he
has written or to the underlying assumptions of his position
to state that he has paid it no attention.

In one important respect Little has been able to read *The
Secular City* according to the author's intention. He has cor-
ectly discerned that the theological heart of its thesis is the

theme of the Kingdom of God. He makes a gratuitous slur upon Cox's use of that theme, however, when he says, "The Kingdom for him is interrelated, if not identical, with the worldwide process of secularization." Cox says quite clearly that the Kingdom is not identical with secularization, although it furnishes the terms by which that process may be understood and responded to by Christians. His own sense of eschatology is firm enough to describe the Kingdom as "in process of realizing itself."

Finally, Little is quite mistaken in raising the cry "Social Gospel" just because the Kingdom is taken seriously and is suggested as the basis for approaching a Christian understanding of social change. H. Richard Niebuhr's *The Kingdom of God in America* shows not only that this has been an enduring theme in American theology but also that different generations have dealt with it differently.

Because Augustine made such full use of the image of the city in formulating his theology at the time of the breakup of the Roman Empire, we would hardly say that Cox is an Augustinian at heart. Neither would we say that the Social Gospel was "Puritan" because it shared the Puritans' reliance on an understanding of the Kingdom of God.

Cox uses both city and Kingdom as images, but he does so in his own frame of reference. *The Secular City* has not "resuscitated" the Social Gospel nor does it employ "almost identical language." The six decades that intervened have made a lot of difference. Harvey Cox, on the evidence of *The Secular City*, understands that difference. It is not so evident that his critics do.

# CHAPTER 6

# Secular Style and Natural Law

## Michael Novak

The brilliant little book by Harvey Cox on secularization may mark a milestone in ecumenical discussion. *The Secular City* celebrates man as man, his world, his tasks, his style, his history. *The Secular City* of pragmatism and profanity seems to be a city of natural law.

To be sure, Cox rejects the phrase "natural law" as characteristic of the mentality of the Town. Moreover, several of the many types of natural-law theory are of a nonhistorical, abstract, immutable sort that are clearly of little use in technopolis. But when the dimension of supernature is collapsed so as to "*coincide*" with the dimension of the profane and when the Christian's task is to "grow to maturity" and to "accept the risk of responsible decision-making," what can one call such an ethic but a new type of natural law?

"Natural law" is to some Protestants as much a red flag as "secularization" is to some Roman Catholics, but for opposite reasons. Some Catholics fear secularization because it means what Cox says it means: a sense of history, a kind of relativity, increasing reliance on individual judgment. Some Protestants fear natural-law theory because it seems to stand so firm against just such realities.

But there is a type of natural-law theory held by some Catholics—to some extent by John Cogley and John Courtney Murray; to a further extent by its historian Dom Odon Lottin and by its theoretician Bernard Lonergan—which contends that natural law is not immutable and "out there" but is developing and intrinsic to man's active and inventive intelligence. There are unchanging *principles* of natural law only in the sense in which *operations of intelligence* are principles, not in the sense in which *propositions,* precepts or premises are principles.

Natural law, according to this theory, is functional. Its roots lie in irrepressible appetites in man's heart and mind: for self-preservation, for endless intellectual inquiry, for social inventiveness and civic conversation, and for the hunt of the hidden God. The operations that formally constitute this natural law are four: experience that raises questions; inquiry that terminates in insight; further inquiry that tests insights against evidence; and decisions whether or not to act according to such experience, insight, and evidence.

Each of these operations, it will be noted, is required for the theology of revolution sketched by Cox. They must be exercised if men are (1) to identify the gap between the new reality and the old; (2) to interpret the failure of some to understand what is happening; (3) to devise strategies to lead such persons to the requisite insights and evidence; and (4) to gain "an understanding of catastrophe." Operations of experience and intelligence clearly mediate all four of these features.

Each of the basic operations, moreover, appears to be accessible to all normal human beings, East or West, Greek or Hebrew, male or female. They might, then, possibly be called "natural" to men—not because they are (particularly the latter ones) statistically frequent but because they are universally accessible.

Moreover, this type of natural-law theory, which we may call the operational type, recognizes the historical conditions under which such operations are performed; it is a natural-law theory for men, not for angels. Consequently, its focus is not upon propositional content or a conceptualized code, both of which are the products of a certain time in history; rather it is upon the set of operations that must be performed before a sound moral judgment can be credited at all.

What is unchanging is the requirement that the set of operations be performed. The material upon which they work, the viewpoint from which they are exercised and the conclusions at which they arrive obviously change. It is plausible that there is a minimum content to natural law—H. L. A. Hart admits as much—sufficient to ensure the possibility of social life and the ability to perform the basic operations. But that is not the fundamental point.

This is not the place for a fuller analysis of the operational type of natural-law theory. With certain qualifications, the thesis has been defended that such a view of natural-law theory best represents the positions of Aristotle (who in the *Nicomachean Ethics* did not use the phrase "natural law") and Aquinas (who in the *Summa Theologica* devoted but one question to natural law in a moral treatise of over a hundred questions). But this nice historical question is not germane, either, and in any case will hardly interest those justifiably anxious to get on with the big cities of the future and less concerned about the small towns of the past.

Moreover, the future is what makes *The Secular City* important ecumenically. One of the greatest drawbacks in Protestant-Catholic discussions is that both groups have heretofore used the same ethical words—"reason," "law," "faith," "love"—with quite different definitions and sociological overtones. *The Secular City* appears to be a further chapter in a line of thought first begun in this country by Reinhold Niebuhr (Cox is the Niebuhr of the present generation); and it will alter the situation in two ways.

In the first place, Cox would have both Catholics and Protestants drop the language of the town, the ethical and theological language of an earlier and departed *manière de vie*. In the second place, he would have Protestants take up the language of the profane world, the language of secular men, the language of intelligence, of human purposes, drives, and needs.

Many Catholics will go halfway. They will not insist on the phrase "natural law." So many things have changed since that phrase first gained currency in their ethical tradition that it is, in any case, dangerously misleading. Harvey Cox has given them the word: "secularization." Natural-law theory has become the theory of the secular style.

However, charity (for Aquinas the "root, mother and form" of all the moral virtues) remains even in the city—that love of the unseen God that is manifested in love of the neighbor seen, even if not a *Thou* and hardly spoken to. Luckily for Catholics, who never manage to change vocabularies as soon or as often as their fellow Christians, *The Secular City* does not require them to abandon that as well.

# CHAPTER 7

# Cox on His Critics

## Harvey Cox

I was awed and a little nonplussed when *Christianity and Crisis* saw fit to devote an entire issue to four readable and provocative reviews of my book *The Secular City*. Indeed I am a little embarrassed that such powerful searchlights and high-gauged weapons have been brought to bear on my tiny flying machine since it was designed as a study book, intended mainly to provoke college students to discussion and not to goad bishops and seminary professors into rebuttal. Nevertheless, I learned a great deal from reading their reviews; and in the interest of moving the discussion farther along, I submit the following rejoinder.

Kilmer Myers finds in my writing an insufficient appreciation for the Catholic understanding of the church, and I am sure he is right. I think this has to do with heredity, but I twitch a little when people say Jesus Christ *is* the Church, mainly because this formula seems to undercut the need for responding to Christ and *following* Christ. It also seems to endanger the Reformation's emphasis on the fact of the church's *own* sinfulness and need to repent. If the church is Christ, and we are the church, then why do we so often betray Him? Still, when Bishop Myers invokes the church as the sacrament of humanity, I get interested and would be willing to have my sectarian prejudices corrected. I agree, in any case, that my view of order in the church and its relation to organization needs considerable strengthening.

That my little book may have altered Paul Lehmann's habits of thinking comes as disquieting intelligence. His thought has had such a germinal effect on the church for so long that I would regret to assume any responsibility for its deflection into some other path. His review was so generous and so favorable, I hesitate to mention the fact that one reason he may have enjoyed the book was that I learned many of the ideas from him. Indeed, it was under his tutelage that I launched out into the crosscurrents and underflows of the (then untranslated) *Kirchliche Dogmatik* of Karl Barth.

Although I have now emerged from that bracing ocean of theological stimulation, much of its salt still clings to my thinking; hence I am not at all unpleased to be adjudged "orthodox" and indeed "Chalcedonian" by Dr. Lehmann (designations that both Bishop Myers and Dr. Little might dispute). I am grateful to Dr. Lehmann for helping me be both orthodox and radical. If my book allows him to let his jangling phone go unanswered with fewer twinges of guilt, this is small recompense for what he has already given me.

Charles West, another theologian upon whose contribution to the theology of secularization I have relied, has spied some Nietzschean currents in my thinking. He may be right, and I would feel more uncomfortable about it had I not just come across this significant passage written by Dietrich Bonhoeffer during his period in Spain in 1929 (the year I was born):

> The Christian stands free, without any protection, before God and before the world, and he alone is wholly responsible for what he does with the gift of freedom. . . . The Christian creates new tables, a new Decalogue, as Nietzsche said of the Superman. Nietzsche's Superman is not really, as he supposes, the opposite of the Christian; without knowing it, Nietzsche has here introduced many traits of the Christian made free, as Paul and Luther describe him (*No Rusty Swords* [New York: Harper, 1965], p. 44).

I would say Bonhoeffer went too far here, but the theological implication of man as a value-*creating* animal does need deeper exploration. This issue and *not* the tiresome debate about "contextual" versus "principial" is central to theological ethics today. If "values" are not eternally fixed but are part of the cultural world man himself creates, where do "good" and "evil" come in? I suspect that for the Christian they come through his call to be the transvaluer of values (another Nietzschean idea), the man who seeks unendingly to humanize the social environments in which he is placed.

At one point, of course, I differ basically with Nietzsche and his modern theological followers. It is not the death of the Wholly Other but a call from him that enables man to become the creator of his own world and city.

This brings me to Dr. West's most telling point: his trenchant reminder that there are times when we cannot create anything, when we can do nothing, when we must "live with insoluble problems without the illusion that some politics or technology can get rid of them." I am sure he is right. He might have also noted, as one thoughtful lay friend did, that my book never mentions death.

What shall I say to this very telling criticism? It is not enough to suggest that Charles West has lived longer and under infinitely more taxing circumstances than I have and could write about things I shy away from dealing with. This is, however, true. He is also writing a book on the theology of the secular, and I am confident that he will be able to include that element of tragedy, of depth, judgment and mystery, that is somehow skimped in mine without sacrificing the basically celebrative mood we would both agree is basic to the Gospel. I look forward to his book.

David Little twits me severely for not coming clean and acknowledging my ancestry in Walter Rauschenbusch and the Social Gospel. Now I am certainly somewhat influenced by Rauschenbusch, as I suppose every young American theologian is. As a matter of fact, I did not rely directly on any of his writings for *The Secular City*, since I was at that time more caught up with the contemporary European interpretations of *"sich realisierende Eschatalogie,"* as my references in Chapter 5 indicate.

(Incidentally, Gerhard Sauter, the young Bonn theologian, has recently shown very convincingly that Bonhoeffer's "nonreligious interpretation" may be traceable to the Kingdom of God theology of Ragaz and Blumhardt, the European contemporaries of Rauschenbusch.)

Also, as George Younger has pointed out, the giant figure of Karl Barth looms between all of us and Rauschenbusch. My emphasis on the initiative of God and on His otherness and my centering of man's responsibility in his election by God all put me a little outside the Rauschenbusch camp as I understand it. The Kingdom of God has been used as the touchstone of various theologies for centuries. Using it today does not automatically render someone a "Social Gospeler."

Still, I am not sure what would happen if I did confess a secret identity with Rauschenbusch, since I detect in Dr. Little's review a certain ambivalence toward the Social Gospel. Does he want to identify me with it so I can be more easily discarded or so that a valuable tradition in American theology may be given its due? In rereading his review I am not clear as to his intention. In any case, since my relationship to that tradition is a somewhat indirect and questionable one, I am afraid he and other readers will have to accept what I say or reject it on its own merits instead of utilizing the timeworn academic technique of identifying it with some other movement for which we have a set of ready-made attitudes and evaluations.

Space forbids a reply to Mr. Novak and other Roman Catholics who have written to me or about my book. Novak's suggestion that *The Secular City* contains a kind of natural-law thinking I find wonderfully provocative. It has forced me to look again, this time expectantly, at a theory I had discarded perhaps much too quickly.

Finally, may I say that although I appreciate the reviews immensely I am sorry they all came (with the exception of Bishop Myers') from professional academics. *The Secular City* is a kind of tract. Or maybe a manifesto. It lacks the careful qualification and cautious provisionality I learned to use in writing seminar papers. I would have appreciated a review or two from inner-city ministers, urban laity, restless college students. People like these are the ones who inspired me to write the book and gave me most of the ideas. It was, and is, mainly for them that the book is intended.

# PART THREE

# The *Commonweal* Debate

# CHAPTER 1

# Toward a Theology of Secularity

## *Daniel Callahan*

Ordinarily, there is nothing so hard for the religious man
to cope with as social change. It sets him to twitching, worry-
ing and desperately attempting to squeeze from Scripture
some measure of solace. Now and then he may try to find a
way of turning the change to his advantage or see some
faintly redeeming possibilities in cultural earthquakes. But his
more common response is denunciation of the new. He feels
threatened, and his instant reaction is defensive and abusive.
Historically, he has some reason to feel this way. Massive
social change inevitably affects the religious life of a society.
The shift from feudalism to capitalism in the West is as good
an example as any of what can happen. Entrepreneurs, not
bishops, began to call the tune. Troubled believers felt they
could only hum a dirge.

Of late there has been a shift in this pattern. During the
past couple of decades one theologian after another has come
forward to reluctantly bless scientific, technological and economic advances. They have learned at least one lesson from
their predecessors' mistakes: no amount of ecclesiastical rail-
ing can do much to stop social upheavals. The way to survive
is to hang on for dear life, all the while looking for some way
of legitimately baptizing the new tiger. The theologian may
not always like what he has to do, but at least he does it. He
smiles bravely and gets to work.

Harvey Cox is very much a part of this new mode, but he
goes one step further, ecstatically hailing contemporary social
change as the occasion for a revitalized Christianity. As much
as anything, it is probably this fetching enthusiasm which

accounts for the reception being given his book *The Secular City*. Eagerly passed from hand to hand and quickly adopted by a variety of study groups, it has all the earmarks of a religious *cause célèbre*. It must, then, be meeting a deep need: the longing for a persuasive and unembarrassed theology of secularity. Many attempts have been made in this direction, but almost all of them suffer from the debilitating drawback of treating secularity as a religious disaster—a redeemable disaster, but still a disaster. There is no hint of this in Cox's book.

The key to its power lies in his almost rapturous love for two characteristic features of our age: secularization and urbanization. This will not commend the book to some, but Cox starts from a premise hard to dismiss: *what is*. Far from running their course, secularity and the city are just beginning to take hold. There are always strategies available to evade the impact of historical trends: one can work for the return of a golden age, or fashion utopias, or just withdraw into private metaphysical enclosures, seeking an otherworldly transcendence. Cox will have none of this. His method is to look squarely in the eye that face of contemporary life which most offends the religious and cultural savants and then to say: you are good, and if you are not we can make you so.

The much-bemoaned anonymity of urban life, for instance, Cox hails. It provides the possibility of historically unparalleled freedom from social convention and culturally enforced mores. Mobility and rootlessness provide a like possibility: a liberation from the smothering embrace of small-town provincialism. Another omnipresent bogeyman of the wise, the modern organization, is no less extolled. Better that we have a structure of human relationships and purposes, with flexibility, secularized goals, orientation toward the future and limited claims upon its members than a sacred order with enslavement to the past and deification of law and custom.

Cox's treatment of "secularization" is unflinching. Defining it as "the liberation of man from religious and metaphysical tutelage, the turning of his attention away from other worlds and toward this one" (p. 17), he defends its human values and claims that its roots are biblical. How is this possible?

Cox's argument rests on three points. There is the disenchantment of nature stemming from the Hebraic conception of creation; the desacralization of politics arising from a separation of the political and religious order; and the deconsecration of values which issues from the Jewish relativizing of human values and their representations. Thus was the way opened for a "constructive relativism," which "allows secular man to note the transience and relativity of all cultural creations and of every value system without sinking into the abyss of nihilism" (p. 33). From these roots the technological-urban tree was able to spring.

The cumulative result is a secular man who is pragmatic and profane: "life for him is a set of problems, not an unfathomable mystery. He brackets off the things that cannot be dealt with and deals with those that can. He wastes little time thinking about 'ultimate' or 'religious' questions. And he can live with highly provisional solutions" (p. 63). Just the kind of man, in other words, who is the despair of Sunday preachers. Not so for Cox, whose book shows the decisive impact of Bonhoeffer. "The Gospel," he writes, "does not call men to return to a previous stage of his development. It does not summon man back to dependence, awe and religiousness. Rather it is a call to imaginative urbanity and creative secularity." Just as the city has replaced the town, so also should the political replace the metaphysical as the context of human thought.

Are there any clouds on the horizon? Very many, but none which are incapable of human mastery given intelligence, planning and the full freedom of the Gospel. The role of the church is not to change the present historical direction of society, but to exercise its power of cultural exorcism, its mission of reconciliation, its potentialities as an avant-garde for the Kingdom of God.

"God"? One might well inquire at this point just how God fits into this secularized world. Having dismissed metaphysics, Cox is not tempted to create a new natural theology. Instead he asserts that the word "God" has no meaning for secular man; and he implies that even the Christian is not very certain what it means. But shouldn't this at least be a source of discomfort, or even of those existential paroxysms which Cox deplores? Not at all, for God has often hidden Himself for a time, choosing to reveal His name only gradually "through the abrasive experiences of social change. . . . Perhaps, like Moses, we must simply take up the work of liberating the captives, confident that we will be granted a new name by the events of the future" (p. 268).

All of this is a rich pudding, especially from a Protestant minister and professor who in an earlier age would have been called a "divine." But it adds up to a coherent whole, however questionable many of the pieces. By and large, it makes considerably more sense than some of the speculation to be found in a recent volume of the *Concilium* series, *The Church and the World*, edited by Johannes B. Metz. This is painful to say, because the purpose of the volume is to chart the new frontiers of Catholic thought. The problem is not that the *Concilium* volume lacks boldness or even originality, but that many of the authors are still too much caught up in metaphysical, existentialist or personalist quandaries.

A reading of Cox's book has *almost* convinced me that the day of such problems has passed. However pertinent for some aspects of human existence, a relentless concentration on them contributes very little to the creation of viable social structures and mastery of the material world. It is to continue, in other terms, the traditional quest for the absolute— whether that be construed as a grasp of the totality of being, the nature of existence or the essence of persons. All too easily this plays into the hands of those who cannot stand the problematical, the functional, the pragmatic, the experimental. They are essentially "religious" searches, at least if religion is understood as a hunt for the permanent in the face of the transitory, of ultimate meaning amidst uncertainty. Too often they are concerns which tend to keep alive some old and dangerous dualities, even if that is not their intention.

The persistence of dualism can be seen in a distinction Monsignor Gerard Philips commends in his essay in "The Church and the World." "Catholics," he says, "are learning to make a clearer distinction between their strictly ecclesial

mission and the mature program of action they have to realize now in the world." Heaven help us if they are. What
Monsignor Philips does not seem to notice is that a sharp
sundering of the spiritual and the temporal leads to an
egregious type of Christian utilitarianism: man should be
served, not for his own sake, but for that of the church. As
he revealingly puts it, the church "could not perform its
primary mission if it did not rouse in its members, in behalf
of all their human brethren, a spirit of disinterested mutual
help." This kind of thinking has been the source of the
church's failure to demonstrate that it is fully able to help
build a humane social order. It is nothing less than a gentle
way of saying that the church's ultimate interests lie elsewhere, thus forgetting that when man is slighted for the sake
of God, God will soon be slighted also.

Equally mistaken, though less hazardous, is Hans Urs von
Balthasar's assertion in the same volume that a "demythologized" and "dephilosophized" theology "would have nothing
more to do with the totality of being." "Of necessity," he
says, "it could only present itself as a solace for the anguished
existential subject." I must confess I cannot discover where
this "necessity" lies. The whole point of trying to rid theology
of dead myths and an excessive dependence upon philosophical modes of thought is to grasp better the essence of the
biblical message in its own terms, and from there to learn
something about man's condition. One major fruit of this
effort has been the discovery that the Bible is far more than
the husk of hidden eternal truths. It is a record of man's
encounter with God, a God who reveals Himself in history
rather than in the philosopher's study, a God who speaks
through the language of events rather than that of timeless
essences.

Put abstractly like this, there are probably few Catholic
theologians who would sharply dissent. I am merely saying
what it has now become fashionable to say. Yet if one looks
to find evidence of a new creativity in dealing with man's
historical and political life, one is most likely to discover only
a new set of abstractions. One might expect, for instance, to
find the Catholic sociologist or psychologist accorded a

stature equal to that of the theologian—or to find the natural
and social sciences, which deal with matter and man in their
empirical grittiness, dominating the advance guard of Catholic thought. This is not the case at all. Most of the great
Catholic figures of our day—the Rahners, the Küngs, the
Schillebeeckxs, the von Balthasars—are notably scant in references to economics, political science, urban planning and
even to the sociology and psychology of religion.

What they have done, and what the Catholic Church has
honored them for, is to substitute new theologies for old
theologies. That is a worthwhile project for those concerned
with the intricacies of the Christian revelation; and some
people should be. But it is also a graphic illustration of why
even the freshest Catholic theology has the same mark of
irrelevance as did its forerunners. It is essentially turned in
upon itself, and nowhere more obvious than when it tries to
talk about "the world" exclusively in the language of theology. The new realm of Catholic thought—of I–Thou encounters, salvation history, omega points, Lonergan-like insight,
*sein* and *dasein*, kerygma—is a delightful place for Catholics
to live. It's just that we're the only ones who live there, along
with a few scattered Protestants. The rest of the world lives
somewhere else, and our new jargon is just as esoteric and
beside the point outside the family circle as the old.

I say this out of a vast sense of frustration. Give or take a
few setbacks, the recent progress of Catholic theological
thought has been nothing less than spectacular. But I see little
evidence that it will come to mean anything more to secular
man than did the old scholastic panoply of clear and certain
ideas. I am secular man, too, and my Catholic brothers are
legion.

In an otherwise excellent article in *America* on Christian
secularity ("The World Is Already Christic," May 29, 1965),
Father Thomas E. Clarke, S.J., felt compelled to caution that
"the distinction between *sacred* and *secular* is beyond question." There we have the central issue: Is this distinction
actually beyond doubt? If it is, then it is almost certainly
hopeless to expect that secular man will ever know what the
Christian is talking about. Equally hopeless would be an ex-

pectation that the Christian secular man could come to know how to construct a coherent human life. As long as he feels that life for him necessarily entails walking some delicate tightrope between the sacred and secular, the natural and the supernatural, the redeemed and the unredeemed, he will always be dizzy. He will not and cannot go off into the desert; but then, he will always worry whether he can be as totally committed to man's life on earth as the most ardent atheist.

I don't think this is a fictitious or outdated problem. Some of the most disturbed Catholics I have run across recently are those who have heeded the Church's call to serve the world and then have found, once they started doing so, that their Christianity ceased to have much meaning for them. They discovered that the work of the world seems to carry its own intrinsic justification, requiring neither religious motives nor religious goals. A shock of this kind is only natural to those exhorted for years to maintain a balance between sacred and secular—and all the more so when they have been told that the secular world has no final meaning.

Far more illuminating is a perspective on God and man which sees man's temporal concerns and drives as one with his spiritual destiny. The central meaning of the Incarnation, I take it, is that Christ *has* redeemed man and matter. If this is so, then the sacred and the secular have entered into a relationship of unity; not a perfect or complete unity, but surely enough to render any talk of their radical difference highly misleading. Worse than that, a desire to maintain the distinction forces one to follow Monsignor Philips' route into the wilderness of primary and secondary ecclesial missions, of separating love of God from love of man. Once into that jungle there is no way out.

Yet Cox's stance has some equally imposing difficulties to overcome. Can secular man, after all, afford to ignore metaphysics? Can he really get away with a purely pragmatic solution to his sociohistorical problems? Up to a point, I think the answer is yes to both questions. It has to be yes, because many men patently manage to live antimetaphysical, pragmatic lives and seem to be none the worse for it. The Christian may look at such a man with skepticism and incredulity, but there are many secular men who can confound his pessimistic expectations.

The question, then, is not whether such men can exist, and exist happily—they just do—but whether mankind as a whole can live this way either now or in the future? Let me say that I personally do not know; it would be silly to say anything else. At the same time, it also has to be said that decisions have consequences. The pragmatic decisions taken by this generation for the sake of its own life will inevitably affect, if not decisively shape, the life of future generations. The past has always imposed its relativities upon the future, and it is likely to continue doing so. The pragmatic man who does not recognize this will be a dangerous man. But as soon as he does see that his decisions will have consequences and tries responsibly to take this fact into account, he will cease to be wholly pragmatic. He will have no other choice. One way or the other, he will have to dip his toe into the murky waters of metaphysics. He will have to fashion at least some tentative conclusions about what is good for man regardless of his specific historical situation. He will have to say what minimal conditions are necessary for human freedom, existence and fulfillment.

Cox would have the Christian "unreservedly contextual" in his ethics and in his evangelism. Yet if the responsible secular man cannot be all that contextual himself, it is difficult to see how the Christian can either. What Cox wants is a Christian who knows how to respond to his present age; how to un-encumber himself of an anachronistic past; how to speak to the here and now; how to lay the ground for the future. These are fine goals, but each of them actually requires the ability to get out of one's context, at least some of the time. Cox himself does this when he speaks warmly of a "biblical perspective" on the world and when he uses the imagery of the "Kingdom of God." These are categories which cut across time and through history. They illuminate the contextual without themselves being wholly contextual.

Ironically, of course, once Cox begins using biblical lan-guage, he cuts himself off from secular man. Here, I think, Cox has to fish or cut bait. If secular man and his way of life are self-sufficient, any talk about taking a "biblical perspective" is beside the point. Who needs it, and so what, anyway? The only possible reason for bothering would be that even at its utopian best the world of secular man will have its nether regions. The *Playboy* bachelor can make the most of urban anonymity; not everyone else can. Mobility is grand if one has brains and a future; not everyone does. And so on. The urban-secular coin has two sides and so does man.

Had Cox recognized this more clearly, he might well have been less cavalier toward those caught up in existential anguish. One reason for their plight is the often oppressive weight of the present. There are times when life is just awful: boring, stupid, brutal or trivial. The promise of the future does not always, nor can it, drive out the pain of the present. Some people are going to die tomorrow. That is their context, and they want to know why. This is a very personal question, not something that history or sociology or politics can throw much light on. A question like this is wretchedly ultimate, direct and noncontextual. It just will not go away.

An obvious conclusion at this point would be to say that the upshot is something of a draw. Those who would have men put aside metaphysics, existentialism and the higher speculations of personalism in favor of politics, sociology and history have the temper of modern man on their side. They are also in a better position to turn directly to immediate human needs, unencumbered by any pressing demand to work out final values and goals. On the other hand, man is not just a political and historical creature; he does not live by social reconstruction alone. Someone has to speak to the nonhistorical self, and never more so than when all of a man's plans and hopes come to nothing or when he looks death in the face. Thus can the ball be volleyed back and forth.

Still, I suspect that a choice has to be made. Ideally, it should be possible for humans to turn their attention simultaneously toward metaphysics and social planning. Psychologically, this is difficult to manage. Historically, the Christian's obsession with ultimacy has meant a debasement of the temporal. Even when he tried to take his present moment seriously, his theological concerns would not allow him to do so. His orientation toward an eternal future kept him in bondage to the historical past; the world was always outrunning him. Once again it is outrunning him. His only hope of catching up, I'm afraid, is to let go. To let go of his desire for immediate meaning. To let go of his wish for religious security. To let go of his need to see the hand of God. To let go of the quest for a new vision, or the revivification of the old one.

I suppose this is almost too much to ask of the Christian. But if the Christian cannot wait for God, if the Christian cannot make the course of history his own, if the Christian cannot give himself unreservedly to man and his temporal existence—then it is hard to see how he will ever live in the present, much less speak to it. There are many ways of gaining the whole world while losing one's soul. There are also many ways of gaining one's soul and losing the world. The world we stand to lose is the world Christ redeemed.

# CHAPTER 2

# An Exchange of Views

*Andrew Greeley*

In his recent article (see pp. 91–100) in which he joins in the chorus of praise for Harvey Cox's best seller, *The Secular City*, Daniel Callahan laments that Catholic theologians do not pay much attention to sociology. For obvious reasons I can but agree with such a profound comment. But theologians like Mr. Cox and Mr. Callahan had better beware; if sociology becomes a *locus theologicus,* the camel will have his nose in the tent and theologians will be forced to argue not only with each other—which is perfectly legitimate sport —but they will also have to argue with obstreperous sociologists who will want to question the sociological assumptions that theologians will be making.

But the fat is already in the fire and it is my intent to question the sociology on which Mr. Cox and Mr. Callahan base their theology itself, which seems to be an Americanized version of Bishop Robinson's marriage of Bonhoeffer and Tillich. If Messrs. Cox and Callahan say that the church can get along with secular man, I am not disposed to argue with them. My problem is not whether religion can live with secular man, but whether he exists; and I will contend that save in senior faculty positions in some universities and in certain places in the communications industry, secular man is not common in the United States and does not seem to be growing more common. On the contrary, secular man is a theologian's romanticized version of mass man—and he doesn't exist either.

To say that man is becoming secular has, it seems to me, taken on at least five different meanings in contemporary writing:

1) Religion is not formally identified with every aspect of human life, as in primitive societies.

2) Man in his public and private life does not live up to the ideals of his religious belief.

3) Religion should not attempt to influence the decisions of civic authority or indeed play any role beyond the spiritual formation of the individual believer.

4) Men are less likely to belong to religious organizations or go to church than they were in the past (let us say a hundred years ago).

5) Religious faith and religious organizations have little (and progressively less) influence over the lives of men and the life of society because man is leaving behind the primordial, tribal, communal *"gemeinschaft"* style of the past.

The first proposition is unquestionably true, but hardly new; it was true even before the birth of Christ. If it is amended to say that religion does not have the direct and intimate relationship with public life that it did in the Middle Ages, the statement is still true but now merely several hundred years old, although it is not immediately clear that this means that religion has less influence. Whether religion was dominating public life or vice versa in the so-called ages of faith is at best a moot point; but I would not immediately agree that the Archbishops of Chicago, New York and Boston have less impact on society today than did the Archbishop of Paris during the Bourbon monarchy.

The second statement is certainly true, has always been and probably always will be, but is hardly sufficient grounds for a new theology.

The third notion is a theological value judgment and may or may not be true, but does not prove that the city is in fact secular.

The fourth proposition is demonstrably false in American society and can hardly be what the neosecularists mean.

So we assume that at least in our discussions with Messrs. Cox and Callahan we are dealing with the secularity described in the fifth proposition. This seems to be legitimate in view of Mr. Callahan's remark "The much bemoaned anonymity of urban life, for instance, Cox hails. It provides the possibility of a historically unparalleled freedom from social convention and culturally enforced mores. Mobility and rootlessness provide a like possibility: a liberation from the smothering embrace of small-town provincialism" (to which an evil but frolicsome spirit in the back of my skull mutters, "Oh yeah? We should have it so good!"). And Mr. Cox himself adds "Every college sophomore knows that modern man is a faceless cipher" (p. 39). (At this the frolicsome spirit goes into peals of laughter about sophomores and their clichés' being used as proof for anything.)

But what other proof do either Mr. Callahan or Mr. Cox offer for their theories of the anomie of modern urban man? Cox quotes T. S. Eliot, Sören Kierkegaard, Ortega y Gasset, Rilke, Franz Kafka and Ferdinand Tönnies; and this, my friends, is the sociological dimension in contemporary theology. We argue to an anonymous, mobile, secularist society on the grounds that everyone knows it exists (including sophomores) and that theologians, philosophers and the literati know it more than anyone else. As to the sociologists who in recent years have thoroughly studied the concept of mass man, well, no one bothers to read them, much less to take them seriously. There is indeed a long sociological tradition about the shift from peasant society to industrial society which in oversimplified fashion is presented to college sophomores and can be taken in its simple-minded version to offer some substance to the assumptions of Messrs. Cox and Callahan. Tönnies called it the shift from *gemeinschaft* to *gesellschaft* (translated frequently into English as "community" and "association"); the followers of Charles Horton Cooley speak of the change from "primary" (intimate, face-to-face) relationships to "secondary" (formal and specific) relationships; Howard Becker wrote of the change from the "sacred" to the "profane"; Robert Redfield used the words "folk" and "urban"; and Talcott Parsons has synthesized all previous theories by developing a series of continua (the number of which changes periodically) between universalistic and particularistic, achieved and ascribed, specific and diffuse modes of behavior.

Common to all the theories is the concept that with the breakup of the peasant village, with its traditional, intimate, family-centered, tribal, static patterns of action, there emerged a radically new kind of human behavior that was formal, contractual, rationalized, impersonal, dynamic and highly individualistic. The assumption of the theorists of mass society (and, by implication, of Messrs. Callahan and Cox) is that this new kind of behavior destroyed the old so that modern man is a mere face in a lonely crowd, living an atomized, detached, alienated, anomic life; *gemeinschaft* is gone, lament the mass-society theorists; for poor modern man there remains only heartless *gesellschaft*. And the secularist theologians arrive on the scene and announce, "How wonderful because man is at last free."

But there is another sociological tradition within which there would be dissent. Scholars in this perspective would not deny the rise of *gesellschaft* and its tremendous importance to modern life. But they would have considerable skepticism about the demise of *gemeinschaft* until they saw convincing proof. They would rather be inclined to suspect that primordial, tribal, nonrationalized behavior has survived in technopolis (Cox's word) and indeed is prospering in its transmuted forms. They would further not to be surprised to find that in the primary group, *gemeinschaft* elements of human behavior are still of decisive importance on many, if not most, occasions.

The Chicago school of sociology, to its credit, never did buy the mass-society theory. Since Robert E. Park took his first hard look at Chicago it became clear to this school that metropolis was not anomic but symbiotic, that the city was made up not of atomized individuals but of hundreds of tightly organized and competing local neighborhood communities. And as far as the large cities in the northeastern and northcentral parts of the country are concerned, no one has ever proved Park wrong, and the surburban migration has, if anything, proved him right. Man's inclination to build up *gemeinschaft* communities as quickly as he can has apparently not abated.

In more recent years, as sociology has turned to the search for proof for the broad generalizations of the past (apparently what Professor John Donovan means by "naïve empiricism"), the tradition of skepticism about "mass society" and "anomic man" has grown stronger. Elton Mayo and his colleagues discovered that production at the Hawthorne plant was determined not by the rationalized schedules of the plant manager but by the informal decisions of the face-to-face friendship groups on the assembly lines. Samuel Stouffer found that the primary motive for courage in combat was loyalty to one's "buddies" in the squad. Shils and Janowitz described how the final breakdown of the *Wehrmacht* came only after the combat soldier lost his personal trust in his noncom. Lazersfeld and Berelson learned that voting decisions were made not by isolated individuals but by groups of people in face-to-face contact with each other. Elihu Katz noted that marketing decisions were also part of a primary-group process and not the result of decisions of individual purchasers. Gerhard Lenski shocked the sociological world by showing how religion was a more important predictor of human behavior than social class. My colleague Alice Rossi discovered that, despite all claims to the contrary, the extended family was still a thriving institution and the image of the isolated nuclear family "going it alone" was sheer romanticism. Herbert Gans and Nathan Glazer and Daniel Patrick Moynihan decided not only that the ethnic group was still very much with us, but that it showed no signs of losing its vitality (and, in another role, Moynihan found that ethnicity could still beat you in an election). In short, weep not for *gemeinschaft*, it is still very much with us; and if Glazer, Moynihan, Lenski and Mrs. Rossi are to be believed, it shows no signs of going away.

My basic objection to the work of Harvey Cox is that *The Secular City* shows no awareness of the existence of this tradition of sociological inquiry or of its implications for urban life. If in some respects the city be more secular than it was, it is also very unsecular. The so-called preurban elements have survived into the urban milieux and will continue to survive. A theology which ignores the vigor of the primordial, elemental, *gemeinschaft* bonds that hold a city together is at best only half an urban theology.

I could be tempted to forgive the sociological naïveté of

*The Secular City* if the author and his admirers gave any signs of looking at American cities the way they really are outside the ivy-covered ivory towers of the theological schools. How anyone could look on Chicago beyond the limits of Hyde Park and argue that the primordial elements of human society—religion very much included—are unimportant, I cannot possibly fathom. The real-estate men are aware of how important religion and ethnicity are in suburban developments and how church construction can shape the formation of a whole community. The politicians know it with their delicately balanced tickets and appointments. The journalists know it with their careful coverage of religious news. The Chicago Commission on Human Relations knows it when priests and ministers are summoned to control potential race riots. The Federal Government knows it when it relies on the advice of religious agencies in the war on poverty. The civil-rights leaders know it with their heavy reliance on clerical leadership. The community organizers know it when they rely on the clergy to be the key people in their efforts.

Even at the university, lectures on religion and classes about it are well attended, large numbers of graduate students are practicing believers and ethnicity, if not religion, is, if my faculty colleagues are to be believed, still an important rallying point for social life. Chicago a secular city? Not the way I see it. It has secularized, formalized, rationalized elements of course, but the tribal, the sacred, the informal, the traditional still seem very strong and, as far as one can observe, are not growing appreciably weaker.

I would suspect that the same thing could be said for most large cities in the country. Los Angeles may be an exception, but if the so-called City of Angels is the secular city of the future, then God help us all.

Nor am I persuaded, for all of our happy talk about the relationship between church and state, that organized religion and religious belief are unimportant on the national scene. It is fashionable in liberal Catholic circles to deny the importance of religious involvement in the civil-rights movement (while at the same time criticizing religious leaders for not being more involved); but Federal officials, who periodically renew their demands that religion produce a national con-

sensus on racial justice (and the war against poverty and any
other cause that the Government thinks might be religious),
are somewhat less skeptical. Nor are the latter necessarily
more naïve. Thadeus O'Brien, in a study of changing attitudes on race, discovered that the strongest predictor of at-
titudinal change was how a respondent answered the question, "Did your minister (or priest) preach in the last several
months on racial justice?" We may claim to have a diaspora
society because such claims make us feel very dynamic and
brave, but it might be more realistic to admit that we have a
multidenominational quasi-official religious establishment
which suits most people just fine.

I do not argue that the situation I am describing is better
for religion than the secular city would be if it ever came into
existence; it might be possible indeed for religion to be much
more dynamic in the secular city. I am simply contending
that the secular city does not exist, and given the human's
tendency to preserve the traditional, the primordial, the supra-
rational elements of his life, the secular city may never exist.
A theology of the contemporary American city cannot presume that secularity is the only major dimension to be dealt
with. Unsecularity is equally important. I further trust that
these comments will not be written off as either "conservative" or "optimistic," words that Catholic liberals are inclined
to use to describe any attempt to get at the facts behind their
sweeping generalizations. The question at issue is not whether
the unsecular city is better than the secular one, but whether
the secular city actually exists and whether secular man is
very common. On the basis of the most recent empirical
sociology it is hard to answer in the affirmative to either question. The city is a dynamic balance of the anonymous and the
tribal, the sacred and the profane, the secular and the unsecular, the rational and the traditional, and the balance does not
seem to be a very precarious one. This may be a more complicated version of the city than that of the mass-society theorists, but it has the advantage of being more in accord with
the facts. It may present a greater challenge to the theologians who are looking for a new vision of the city, but if
theologians are going to play the game of using sociology as a
jumping-off point, they had better be warned in advance that

simple and uncomplicated sociological generalizations are usually the kind not yet tested by the collection of facts.

The question still remains as to why sober and perceptive men would be swept along by a view of the city which is at such variance with both sociological data and the readily observable phenomena of city life. It may be in part that their own environment at the upper levels of university life or in the mass media is peopled by a far higher proportion of secular men than is the rest of the republic, although it is not clear either that the universities are as secular as some deeply religious observers think they are or as some senior faculty members would like to believe. Indeed, it seems to me that some of the senior faculty members are not so secular as they would like to have us believe.

The vision of the secular city is also tempting because it sweeps away many of the complexities of the past and offers promise of a brave new beginning. The "God is dead" approach to theology sounds dramatic and dynamic and missionary and fearless. The traditions of the past are gone and now we can bear witness in truly evangelistic fashion in a society where man is at last free from "small-town provincialism" (one might almost add, "from the human condition"). Black is black and white is white and a new era of the Gospel is about to begin in the cold clear light of the secular city. How stirring! How exciting! How romantic! And how wrong. The past is still with us, the city is still complicated, man is still narrow and provincial and traditions still burden us and on occasions enlighten us. How dull. But how true.

So by all means let there be a dialogue between sociology and theology. But if theologians are to make use of sociology in their speculations, then let it be the most recent and the most factual and the most sophisticated sociology and not the popularized, romanticized, sentimentalized sociology of the college sophomore.

## Michael Novak

Those who belong to traditional religious communities are undoubtedly undergoing a spiritual crisis, and it is probably a crisis of culture rather than of faith. One may, however, agree with the way in which Messrs. Callahan and Cox state the problem without agreeing with the direction in which they turn in seeking a solution.

The radical issue is to decide what religion is. Since we have never experienced pure, unacculturated religion, but only religion as it has been incarnated in various forms of Jewish, medieval Catholic, and modern Protestant cultures, no one of us seems very certain about what is transitory in religion and what is indispensable.

Both Cox and Callahan, it seems to me, speak mainly from within the tradition of the secular enlightenment and modern Christianity. Bonhoeffer himself explicitly traces his intellectual lineage in *Letters and Papers from Prison*; it is the tradition of the Enlightenment. The notions of "reason" acceptable within this tradition make inevitable the disparagement of metaphysical inquiry and a radical misunderstanding of alternative traditions. Both Cox and Callahan reflect a widespread contemporary disdain for metaphysics, its "dead myths," and useless "quandaries." In this way they are without question representative of the present conventional wisdom of the leading secular community.

But in a pluralistic society, one need not be abashed by the present conventional wisdom. Any well-developed, sophisticated viewpoint is bound to seem irrelevant to those who do not take the trouble to acquire the experiences, attain the series of insights, and achieve the expertise of concrete judgment required for the mastery of the viewpoint. I have recently spent three years trying to acquire the horizon of contemporary Anglo-American philosophy and another two years trying to enter the complex horizon of American Protestant thought which Cox outlines in his article. When I first undertook these studies, I could not for the life of me understand what lecturers or writers were saying, or why they thought important some of the things which excited them, or why they dismissed some matters (which seemed to me significant) without argument.

Moreover, I think I have learned that there is no such thing as "the wholly secular man"—an abstraction—but only very many individual secular men. In a pluralistic society, each one of them finds himself a member of various minority groups, and each of these groups has an argot and viewpoint of its own which seems irrelevant to other minority groups.

Again, part of the irrelevance of religious language and religious thought which both Cox and Callahan correctly observe seems to me due to the fact that the American educational system, on the university level as well as in the lower grades, allows our people to grow up religiously illiterate. Such students are unable to distinguish authentic religion from the cultural forms which presently go by the name of "religion." Cox is correct when he says that the vast majority of Americans probably regard religion as exactly the kind of phenomenon which Bonhoeffer rejects. But I do not think you can cure that problem with semantics—preaching a "religionless" Christianity—nor with an effort to become "wholly secular."

Callahan questions the distinction between the sacred and the secular, then goes on to employ it; and I think he accepts too uncritically the purported sharp distinction between (all?) modes of philosophical thought and (all?) modes of biblical thought. Catholic scripture scholars, reacting against the Cartesian scholasticism of the seminaries, frequently accept that distinction as a polemical device, but it seems to me that current scholarship is increasingly calling it into question. This difference between Callahan's intellectual approach and my own is basic. I think his approach results from his greater commitment to the modern philosophical tradition and his failure to find in any of his encounters with scholasticism, metaphysics, or even existentialism and personalism, anything that can be "understood" from within the horizon more familiar to him. Consequently, his criticism of other modes of thought seems to me representative of one tradition —presently the leading tradition in American schools—rather than able to penetrate other traditions and to understand them from within.

Above all, I think he underestimates the resources of several strands in the Catholic tradition. Saint Thérèse of Lisieux understood quite well what it is to live "on the borders of unbelief, doubt, and heresy." Her entire mature life was a night of faith. She also understood the fact that every single object, event, and person is *both* secular and sacred; nothing is merely religious, or, on the other hand, religionless. To feed another man is a secular act. It is also a religious act. Only the point of view changes, not the empirical facts. Those disturbed Catholics of whom Callahan writes are wrong if they are looking for their Christianity to knock them over with its "relevance." All it offers is a point of view, a horizon, within which the most wholly secular act imaginable is also imaginable as a symbol of one's love for God, reverence for other men, sense of personal inadequacy or personal gifts, etc. Many Catholics (and Protestants) are disturbed, but perhaps because they have not penetrated into the riches of their own faith—as people like Dorothy Day, for example, have. Grace does not operate in a vacuum, and where there is no effort of imagination and faith the sacred slips from view. Faith is not "given" as facts are given, but as grace is given.

Moreover, in three respects the authentic teaching of Aquinas is secular in the sense required by Cox: (1) his ethics, despite the clear and certain laws laid down by legalistic scholastics, is based on the notion of practical wisdom and singular, contingent, individual decisions; (2) his theory of grace respects the integrity of natural things, which are to be celebrated for their own sakes, and, moreover, does not picture man's action and God's action as in competition; he does not try to "make room for" God; and (3) his theory of the meaning of the word "God," despite conventional misrepresentations of it, does not imply that God is known because He is needed to function in our scientific theories or in the dramatic plot of our lives as some *deus ex machina*. Silence about a hidden and unimaginable God is fitting, but sometimes the human being must speak, and then it is good to have precedents with technical sophistication concerning at least some of the mistakes to be avoided.

The Catholic tradition has a great deal to say on the problem of secularization, partly because it was not as deeply involved as Protestantism in the religion of the modern age, and partly because it has already undergone so many cultural transformations and thus has had to exercise a working theory of transcultural interpretation. Lonergan has been trying to make that theory explicit.

I agree with Callahan that even present-day Catholic thought does not mean much to secular men. For one thing, linguistic, analytic, and pragmatic philosophy are practically virgin territory for such Catholics as come to them aware of other ways of doing philosophy; there has been very little dialogue of the sort believing and nonbelieving existentialists and phenomenologists have been able to conduct in Europe. In the United States, the intellectual gap between the secular and the Christian world has been extraordinarily wide; but dialogue is a two-way street, and the task of entering a highly developed horizon different from one's native horizon requires the expenditure of sweat, blood, and abundant mental self-criticism, which those who are complacent are unlikely to think worth the candle.

Finally, I think the three criteria which Cox ventures as a way of beginning to speak of God to "secular man" are too loosely drawn. For the church of medieval Christendom was (1) undivided in faith; (2) supremely political, effective both in the "spiritual" and in the "temporal" domain; and (3) all too willing to make ethical pronouncements which were concrete and specific. The problem of incarnating Christianity in the social fiber of a new kind of secular culture is an old one, but in noticing the new aspects in our present version of the problem we ought to learn as much as we can from the solutions which preceded ours.

In closing, I am prepared to admit that "the world" is not one part of the mission of the church, but rather that the church is just one small part of the mission to the world, which was given to Christ by Him who "so loved the world." But I do not think that the essence of the church consists *only* in its engagement with the world. Love of God and love of neighbor are so intimately related that the surest proof of the first is the concrete achievement of the second, but the two loves are not totally identical. If it is a mistake to separate the temporal and the eternal according to the perennial tendency of platonic Christianity, and if it is impossible to "synthesize" the two perspectives by setting them side by side, it is likely that an adequate eschatology will provide a thoroughgoing way of celebrating the contingent course of history and, nevertheless, standing under the judgment of a hidden, sometimes apparently cruel, transcedent God, Who at a point in time entered history to say that, despite appearances, He loves. We do not "need" God, but we are privileged to understand that our destiny is not exhausted by the beauties and labors of building the secular city.

## Harvey Cox

Naturally I am very pleased that my book *The Secular City,* has elicited responses from such a respected sociologist as Father Andrew Greeley and such a stimulating critic as Michael Novak. Let me deal with them in turn.

I am delighted that Father Greeley believes, with me, that a searching conversation between theologians and sociologists on the role of the church in contemporary urban society is imperative. I only regret that he has somehow misread much of the intention of my book and that most of this reply must be given over to clarifying misinterpretations. This unfortunately cuts down on the space left for the kind of substantive dialogue from which both of us, I am sure, would profit.

Father Greeley devotes half of his article to refuting what he calls the "mass man" and "mass society" sociologists. He never actually names these culprits so I presume he must mean such writers as William Kornhauser and Bernard Rosenberg, but at one point he seems to imply that Tönnies, Cooley, Becker, Redfield and Talcott Parsons also run with the mass-society pack. I hope he does not mean this since they would all be very uncomfortable with that appellation. Father Greeley does indicate that the common assumption of these unidentified "mass-society theorists" is that "modern man is a mere face in a lonely crowd."

Now, since I do not hold that assumption (indeed, much of *The Secular City* is devoted to attacking it), and since I profoundly disagree with what I understand to be "mass-society" theorists, Father Greeley's ringing refutation of them simply goes by me altogether and our dialogue never gets going. Sometimes I suspect that a less hurried reading of my

book might have enabled Father Greeley to husband his telling polemical energy for a worthier target. Let me show what
I mean by a couple examples of his having overlooked or
misconstrued my case.

Father Greeley's error in identifying me with the "mass-
society" socioloigists derives from a strange misreading of a
phrase (*The Secular City,* p. 39) that "every college sophomore knows that modern man is a faceless cipher." Contrary
to what Father Greeley believes, however, I exhibited this
trite sophomore cliché *not,* as he seems to think, to *prove*
modern facelessness but precisely to reveal the sophomoric
banality of such accusations and to try to arrive at a more
accurate view of modern urban man. Not one to understate
his position, Father Greeley returns no less than four times to
this hapless sophomore and the (admitted) silliness of prov-
ing anything on the basis of what sophomores say. I am sorry
Father Greeley missed this point. It has been a perfectly
evident one to most readers, which is no surprise since on the
same page, only nine lines later, I insist that such sophomoric
ideas are "cheapened and trite."

But Father Greeley seems to be one of those no-nonsense
sociologists with whom one cannot risk very much subtlety in
elucidating an argument. Perhaps the fault is mine, and if I
want to be understood by sociologists, I should in the future
sternly avoid even a smidgin of irony.

Still, if the point about the sophomore with his faceless
urban man escaped Father Greeley, his next misreading is
harder to chalk up simply to the sociologist's tightly disciplined respect for the literal. He goes on to support his assertion that I belong to the popularized and sentimental "mass-
society" sociologists by recalling that in order to prove my
case, "Cox quotes T. S. Eliot, Sören Kierkegaard, Ortega y
Gasset, Rilke, Franz Kafka and Ferdinand Tönnies." He
clinches his indictment by adding ". . . this, my friends, is the
sociological dimension in contemporary theology."

It is true that I quote or refer to these worthy gentlemen.
But what Father Greeley fails to say, or perhaps did not
notice, is that I quote them not to prove my case but *in order
to differ with them.* All these writers represent, sometimes
admittedly with eloquence and intelligence, a view of modern

urban society which my whole book seeks to criticize. Once again our dialogue is frustrated.

But let us press the search for a real issue between us.

Father Greeley seems clearly to have strong likes and dislikes among schools of sociology. He apparently has small regard for the Cooley-Becker-Redfield group with whom he links Mr. Callahan and myself. I admit that I have learned a lot from reading the works of these men although I disagree in important respects with all of them. But surely Father Greeley is too hasty in calling them "popularized, romanticized, sentimentalized." Father Greeley's own preference is for what he calls the "Chicago school," but he also makes room for Mayo, Shils, Stouffer, Lenski and others. Again these are all competent sociologists from whose work I have greatly profited. Yet, for some reason, Father Greeley believes I have "no awareness" of this sociological tradition. He demonstrates my ignorance of them by suggesting that if I were aware of them I would certainly know that "preurban elements have survived in the urban milieu" and that "the tribal, the sacred, the informal, the traditional still seem very strong," and that ". . . primordial, tribal, nonrationalized behavior has survived in technopolis (Cox's word). . . ."

I introduced the word "technopolis" on page 5, a page which Father Greeley seems to have read. But then, on page 6, I wrote, "Nor is tribalism merely a historical category. Even today . . . we find residents of New York City with a tribal mentality . . . We are all tribal, town and technopolitan to some degree." But I am not sure Father Greeley read page 6.

Of course our modern cities are a mixed bag of tribal and technopolitan, preurban and urban components. I never said that secularity is "the only major dimension" of the city, just that it is the newest, the most baffling and seemingly the hardest to cope with theologically.

I am sorry that either my inexact writing or Father Greeley's hurried reading of *The Secular City* has delayed a needed conversation on the real issues of the book. There are things on which I think we could converse profitably. For example:

1) I would be tempted to ask Father Greeley how anyone

who, like himself, is pledged to "the most factual and most sophisticated sociology" and is tenaciously opposed to unfounded generalities can be so sure about what will happen in the future. Though we agree that preurban elements do survive in today's technopolis, how can he be so sure, on a strictly factual basis, that they "will continue to survive"? I would agree with him that "the secular city does not yet exist" (as I say on page 6 of *The Secular City*), but how can he be so sure that it never will?

2) This leads to what I suspect would be the major difference between us. In Greeley's brief paper, I sense an unarticulated but operative theory of social stasis. He sees the city as made up of symmetrically stable components of the religious and profane, rational and traditional, sacred and secular. "The city," says Greeley, in the sentence that comes closest to revealing his own covert social theory, "is a dynamic balance."

Here, then, is a kind of homeostatic theory, very common in contemporary sociology, but certainly not beyond criticism. The critics of homeostatic theory say that although it makes sense of systems and stability in a society, it has trouble dealing with authentic change and newness. Some of its critics would even maintain that homeostatic social theory betrays a conservative ideological bias. It can be used to rationalize stability and status quo, to oppose change.

There are sociologists, however, and in one sense Max Weber (hardly a sentimental sophomore) is their progenitor, whose theory of society is based on linear change moving in a particular direction. Some would speak of this elemental change as "differentiation"; others as "rationalization"; still others as "secularization." Using this type of theory, it would be possible, at least, to make a case for the thesis that preurban patterns *are* diminishing in importance in modern society, that "development" or even "social evolution" do provide more adequate models than "balance" for understanding our world, especially when we see it in historical perspective.

I think Father Greeley and I would undoubtedly disagree on whether urbanization and/or secularization can serve as liberating tendencies. He seems very convinced that they do not, although his expressed basis for this opinion ("Oh yeah?

We should have it so good!") falls somewhat short of the sophistication and factuality he expects in others. Here, I think, he, not I, is the romantic. Despite the enormous problems and obvious dangers of urban civilization, I still contend that the widened range of choice it offers people, in marriage partners, work opportunities and moral options, provides the possibility of an immensely expanded freedom for man. It is our misuse of the gift of urban life and our denying it to certain people that I would oppose, not the essentials of urban life itself.

Incidentally, Father Greeley's foray into a sociology-of-knowledge inquiry as to how Mr. Callahan and myself, both "sober and perceptive" men, can be so wrong-headed also goes somewhat astray. He attributes our puzzling density to our environment at the "upper levels of university life or in the mass media." I am embarrassed to admit in public that for me, at least, this is not quite the case. Although I do teach at Harvard, I have been there now for only six weeks, not quite enough time to reach "the upper levels" (though I was privileged to shake hands with President Pusey at a reception two weeks ago). Besides, I reside and write (and think) not in Cambridge, but in Roxbury, Boston's diminutive Harlem. I believe I feel and experience the city, with all its bewildering problems and its exciting possibilities, with all its contradictions and complexities, just as directly as Father Greeley does. Mr. Callahan will have to answer himself for the degree of secularity up there at the ethereal pinnacle of the mass media where he and his fellow *Commonweal* editors are perched.

There are many points at which I would hope further conversation between Father Greeley and myself would result in agreement. I am sure that we would both confess that the dilemma of how to preserve what is humanizing and enriching from our religious and ethnic traditions while discarding those elements which dwarf and divide us is a crucial problem for urban living today, one for which there is no pat formula. Needless to say, as a theologian I long to find ways to unlock the treasures for our common Christian tradition without returning to the tribalism in which our various denominations were once enmeshed.

Finally, the problem of a "nonreligious" interpretation of the Gospel is far too complex to deal with here. We have come from a period in which Christianity was thought of as the true or highest religion into a period in which such men as Karl Barth, Paul Tillich and Dietrich Bonhoeffer suggest that the Word of the Gospel must be first of all a word *"against"* religion." I am not persuaded that the Christian critique of religion will result in a fully "postreligious age," but surely we cannot simply assume, without hard theological analysis, that the Gospel must always wear a "religious garb," as Bonhoeffer called it. We must not give up the task of trying to do what he called speaking "in a secular fashion of God" just because it seems difficult. Meanwhile, my own affirmation of Christian secularity could be summed up in these words of Pierre Teilhard de Chardin: "In the name of our faith, we have the right and duty to become passionate about the things of the earth."

Michael Novak's criticism is also concerned with the nature of "religion" and its relationship to the Gospel. I would defend the need to extricate the Gospel from "religion," but only if Bonhoeffer's definition of the term "religion" remains constant in the discussion, *i.e.*, religion as dependency, inwardness and a metaphysical perspective which sees *this* world (or "horizon," to use Mr. Novak's Husserlian terminology) somehow subsumed within another one. Against this kind of "religion" the Gospel calls man to maturity, away from a fascinated obsession with his own soul and toward *this* world and this *saeculum* as the appropriate sphere of Christian existence. If another definition of religion is introduced, then naturally the discussion shifts ground. Unfortunately, though Mr. Novak uses the term "religion" repeatedly, he never does tell us what he means by it and this complicates the task of replying to him.

Now for some points of disagreement with Novak: In tabbing Bonhoeffer as a child of the Enlightenment, I believe Mr. Novak has oversimplified a man of highly subtle and broadly inclusive intellectual lineage. Bonhoeffer did respect the Enlightenment more than most theologians, including Mr. Novak, do. But he was also, and I would say even *more*, a son of the Reformation and an heir of the Christian humanism of the Renaissance. Like Pico della Mirandola, Bonhoeffer celebrated the dignity of man as the crown jewel of God's creation. Like Luther, he opposed any good work as a precondition of God's unbounded grace, even if it be the good work of somehow making oneself religious. Bonhoeffer's theology, as Gerhard Ebeling has pointed out, is vigorously and implacably *Christological.* In Him, God, as it were, becomes "secular." It is Jesus Christ, God's secular event, which requires a secular interpretation. I think the Incarnation, not the Enlightenment, is really the key to Bonhoeffer's thought.

Mr. Novak concedes that Callahan and Cox have put the finger on the "conventional wisdom" of the day. He rightly contends that there are other viewpoints one could have, given the time and inclination to develop them. But this is just the point. The church is called to proclaim the word of God in, with and under the thought forms and symbol patterns of its day. We have already learned to communicate the Gospel more or less adequately in the idiom of Aristotelian and scholastic metaphysics and in the argot of idealism and maybe even existentialism. But this will not suffice today. Many of our technically and politically oriented men will not hear the kerygma unless we do the same thing for the emerging world views of our period. This does not mean we simply swallow some new *Weltbild* whole any more than Saint Thomas collapsed before Aristotle or Tillich surrendered to existentialism. The Christian transforms culture by plunging fearlessly into its metaphors and thought processes.

Our situation today is not, however, just the same old need to "incarnate Christianity in the social fiber of a new kind of secular culture." The culture into which the church came in the late Hellenistic period was not a "secular" culture in our modern sense. It was a sacral culture. But ours is not. Ours is a differentiated and radically pluralistic society very different, I think, from anything we have seen before. I believe the secularization process which has brought us here is the fruit, in part at least, of the Christian Gospel and its impact on the West. To me, secularization means (as I wrote in *The Secular City*) "man turning his attention away from worlds beyond and toward this world and this time." Of course there have been notable secular individuals in the past. The colorful thirteenth-century emperor, Frederick II (*"Stupor Mundi"*) is one of my favorites. But such people were exceptions and only in our time do we see a whole cultural *manière d'être* arising which can be called "secular."

Now admittedly there is no "wholly secular" man or society, and the new mood is a vastly difficult one to measure or quantify. But that does not make it any less important or any less real.

Finally, just turning our attention toward this world is not, in itself, a good thing. One can turn toward the world to exploit it, to debase it or to serve it. The Christian turns toward this world because God does in Jesus Christ, and he does so for the same reason, to "love it and give himself for it." The fashioning of a new secular piety will be difficult, but we are not totally devoid of precedents. The worker priests, Simone Weil and Bonhoeffer himself provide provisional models. Georges Bernanos once said, "When I shall be dead, tell the kingdom of the earth that I have loved it much more than I ever dared to say." This articulates the style of the secular Christian better than anything I could write myself.

## Daniel Callahan

Once upon a time I was intimidated by criticisms of the kind Father Greeley has leveled. Here is the professional sociologist bearing down on the amateur, a sword in one hand, a knife in the other and at his back a legion of names, citations and statistics. To the uninitiated, the prospect is appalling. Not only does one face the actual loss of all serious standing, but also he has to suffer the fantasies visited upon amateurs, notably of being "found out" by one's betters, of imagining oneself covered with shame and the object of secret snickers.

However, my early fantasies have disappeared. I discovered that the real issue is not just whether one is competent in sociology, but also whether one accepts some favored sociological schools, names and data. If one does not, but opts for other sociological trends and statistics, the label of "naïveté" is quickly bestowed. This can be very educational, and I have learned much from such criticisms, but it might be well to observe that sociologists fight furiously among themselves over most of the issues under discussion here. Lord knows what kind of fantasies *they* must have.

All of this is by way of saying that I am impressed with Father Greeley's sociological arguments but do not feel demolished. I did not contend (and as Mr. Cox shows, neither did he) that the secular city is triumphant or that secular man is the only man of our day. I will only contend that he is beginning to make his appearance; that he seems to me the logical outcome of modern history and hence to be expected; and that, if Christianity can cope with him, it may find in the world which he will make a setting of unparalleled value for the proclamation of Christ. Father Greeley pertinently observes that there are many countersigns. He is correct, but my own observations tend to support those sociologists who see some significant changes taking place.

Mr. Novak also underestimates the magnitude of the changes taking place. He argues, with notable serenity, that the "Catholic tradition has a great deal to say on the problem of secularization." I do not doubt this—I myself make use of certain strands in the tradition—but I am equally impressed by the uniqueness of the present historical moment and the need for fresh approaches. For me, this means that it is just as important to press original lines of inquiry, to look for new problems and questions, as it is to probe the tradition for past insights. Both tasks are required, but I think the emphasis should fall at the moment on an attempt to find what is unique and different in the contemporary cultural transformations. My own reading of history convinces me that a major reason why the church has been slow to respond to cultural change is that it mistakenly thought, at the outset of revolutionary upheavals, that it knew all the answers, that the "Catholic tradition" had already solved all possible problems. I am sure this is not Mr. Novak's position, but when he insists on the richness of the tradition, he makes it appear that nothing really new can come upon the scene.

At the same time, I think he underestimates the uniqueness of Christianity. He says, for instance, that "all [Christianity] offers is a point of view, a horizon . . ." This seems to me wholly inadequate, neither rich or strong enough to take account of Christ's absolute demands and self-revelation, nor discriminating enough to distinguish Christianity from a philosophical or ideological world view. To commit oneself to Christ is not just to achieve a "point of view" or a means whereby we can imagine different acts in different ways. If, as much contemporary work on faith and Christology argues persuasively, faith essentially is trust in the person of Jesus Christ, a relationship of love and hope, then it is highly misleading to translate this faith without remainder ("all") into the language of "horizon" and "point of view." Those analytic philosophers whom Mr. Novak implies I love just a bit too much would call this a "category mistake." It is, I think, possible to see a new horizon as a consequence or an unfolding of one's faith in Christ, but I think it seriously mistaken to confuse this possibility with the faith itself.

One of the great values of Bonhoeffer is that he tried to take us away from mistakes of this kind. "Religion" supplies us with a "point of view," answers our questions about existence, fulfills our needs. But Bonhoeffer was saying that Chirst gives us something even better: Himself. Moreover, Christ can give something to that consummate man of our age, the "man who has everything." "Religion," by contrast, can only give something to those who have nothing or very little; it begins to fail when men are able to fashion a meaningful horizon of their own making. That is why Bonhoeffer's point about a "religionless" Christianity is more than a matter of semantics —and why Mr. Novak's "horizon" may seem a very insipid dish to an emergent secular man.

I think Mr. Novak has misread some passages of mine when he speaks of my "failure to find in any of his encounters with scholasticism, metaphysics, or even existentialism and personalism, anything that can be 'understood' from within the horizon more familiar to him." On the contrary, I have received almost all of my major orientations, concepts and interests from these encounters. From my exposure to what Mr. Novak calls "the presently leading tradition in American schools" I have received far less, mainly an interest in language and the logical structure of various modes of discourse. I am not, then, criticizing one tradition by means of another, but rather trying to apply what I have learned from the "presently leading tradition" to that which has shaped, formed and nurtured me: scholasticism, personalism, etc. The only qualification I would make here is to say that I have never found metaphysics a very illuminating business; but that, I would suspect, is a personal quirk on my part, long antedating my introduction to the Anglo-Saxon intellectual tradition.

What does distress me—and that was the point of my references to personalism, etc., in my article—is that I and other Christians like me can move easily in that world but it seems to mean no more to secular man than the old manual theology did. Many of the most recent insights of Christian thinkers have meant much to Christians but just about nothing to anyone else. This leads me to think that we may not be asking the right kinds of questions, or that the kinds of interests we Christians are prone to have may render us inept and unskilled in dealing with the real problems of real men.

Here is a question I have often asked myself: Is it possible that the Christian and specifically Catholic tendency to want ultimate answers, to get to the nature of things, is in itself a primary obstacle to dealing effectively, rapidly and imaginatively with social and political problems? I have asked myself this kind of question because of a persistent discomfort when I hear most of the standard explanations as to why Catholics have not been in the forefront of social movements and social change. It is said that the trouble lies not in metaphysics, but in a faulty metaphysics; not in theology, but in a defective theology; not in philosophical anthropology, but in a bad anthropology. There is, to borrow again an expression from the analysts, a clear "family resemblance" in these explanations: whatever the field, they tend to run along the same lines. One cannot very well argue against explanations of this sort since they all depend on the faith that better things can be produced; and who can say they won't be? But one can well inquire whether the traditional Catholic tendency to give first place to metaphysical, theological and anthropological questions is not one reason why social and political problems have always been accorded a derivative importance and why man's temporal life has never been taken with full seriousness—not seriously at all sometimes.

Perhaps we have assumed all too blithely that if we can solve the larger questions of life and death we can then move easily toward a solution of the lesser questions of food, clothes, shelter and social justice. In fact, the shift is not so easily made. Two very different ways of thinking, framing questions and acting come into play. One reason I am attracted by Cox's suggestion that we try casting out theological thought in political and sociological, rather than metaphysical or existential, terms is that we might be in a better position to make the shift. We will then have been trained, in the first place, to deal with man's concrete life rather than being forced, as we are now, to move from one dimension of thought to another, very different, one. Ultimate questions are by no means useless or meaningless or hopeless. But perhaps we have allowed ourselves to become obsessed with them. That is really all I wanted to say in my article.

## Andrew Greeley Replies

Harvey Cox is a man with whom it is a pleasure to do business. In a world where it is difficult to find anyone who will engage in an honest argument, Mr. Cox is only too willing to argue and for this I salute him.

But he is wrong in thinking that our differences can be traced to a hasty reading of his book (I could counter that any reading of my comment which would have me say that Cooley, Becker, and Redfield were "popularized, sentimentalized and romanticized" is pretty hasty, too.) The issue between us is not whether the secular city yet exists but whether it is in the process of coming into existence. Mr. Cox must think that it is; otherwise he would not write a book about and attempt to develop a theology for the typical native of it. Nor do I think that the great popularity of Mr. Cox's book has anything to do with a possible advent of secular man at some time in the future but rather with the belief that he is already on the scene. To this I am forced to reply that contemporary sociology does not, in my judgment, offer much proof for either the man or the city.

Mr. Cox wonders how I can be sure that the secular city will never exist. I cannot, of course, but I think the more appropriate question is how can he be sure that it *will* come into existence. Only God knows the future (if He be permitted to come back from the "vacation" on which some of Mr. Cox's theological colleagues have apparently sent him); the theologian and the sociologist must project present trends into the future and the present trends that social science observes do not, it seems to me, give us much reason to think that detribalization and desacralization are going ahead at a rapid pace. I wonder if Mr. Cox would subscribe to Mr. Callahan's notion that secular man is the "logical outcome of modern history." If he does, then his reasons for accepting the inevitability of the secular city are clear; and so are the differences between us. I am not sure what a "logical outcome of history" is but I suspect that it is a kind of surrogate God which has been invented to replace the real One while he is on vacation; but I don't believe in "logical outcomes of history." On the contrary, I think that the graveyards of intellectual history are littered with the bones of theories about the "logical outcome of history"— including the quaint notion of Herr Professor Karl Marx that there was going to be a proletarian revolution. I will believe that modern man is being progressively desacralized in industrial countries and detribalized when I see empirical proof of this and not before.

Mr. Cox is very wrong if he thinks that I question the tribalism when he says that "Even today. . . we find residents of New York City with a tribal mentality." If he had said that most of the citizens of New York have a tribal mentality which shows no particular signs of going away, I would have no disagreement with him, but I suspect that he would have to design a rather different theology for this tribalized metropolitan than the one he offers in *The Secular City*.

Mr. Cox is very wrong if he thinks that I question the liberating influence of urbanism. Surely no intellectual descendant of Robert E. Park would possibly do this. I am fully prepared to concede that "urban civilization . . . provides the possibility of an immensely expanded freedom for man." But I think this freedom has occurred not so much by secularization of man, but rather by transmuting the primoridal and sacral ties which bind men together into different forms.

Indeed I would contend that the very freedom of which Mr. Cox speaks is made possible to some considerable extent by the social support provided by these transmuted forms of the sacral and the tribal. I am not a theologian, but I should think that theologians would be fascinated by the possibility that some of the new forms of the sacred make the secular feasible.

Nor am I a proponent of any static theory of society; with Mr. Cox I believe in linear change; but I think that it is extremely important whether you call this change "differentiation" (as does Talcott Parsons) or "secularization" as does Mr. Cox. In the Parsonian view religion still plays a crucial role in human life and it is not necessary or even possible to serve up a theology for unreligious man. In Mr. Cox's view, religion is a waning influence and as the process of change goes on it does become necessary to devise a religion for the unreligious. Here is, I take it, the precise point of difference between myself and Mr. Cox, but here we had better leave it in the present correspondence because the difference between a "differentiation" theory and a "secularization" theory would be beyond the scope of an "exchange of views." I would note, however, that the differentiation view which holds that religion still has an immensely important though indirect role to play in modern society would be more in harmony with the writings both of the psychoanalysts and the historians of religion, such as Mircea Eliade, about the persistence of the sacred and the symbolic in the human unconscious.

But if it is a pleasure to argue with Mr. Cox it is impossible to argue with Mr. Callahan. His tools are of the sort that makes dialogue with a good number of *Commonweal* writers impossible: personality arguments, vague references to other "sociological trends and statistics" (without ever mentioning who constitutes these other "schools, names and data"), and outright irrelevancies (the issue is whether the particular change called "secularization" is in fact occurring and whether it is some kind of "logical outcome of history"). Mr. Callahan clearly does not want to argue and so I will not argue with him.

# PART FOUR

# PRESSING THE INQUIRY FURTHER

# CHAPTER 1

# Cox's Vision of the Secular City

## Richard L. Rubenstein

Harvey Cox is a disciple of Dietrich Bonhoeffer. Like his spiritual master he is preoccupied with the problem of how we speak of God without religion. This question haunts *The Secular City*. I would like to suggest that the real question is not how we speak of God without religion, but how we speak of religion in the time of the "death of God."

Religious intellectuals should be profoundly indebted to Professor Cox for his forthright attempt to explore the theological significance of the modern metropolis. One need not agree with Cox's method or his conclusions to recognize the enormous importance of his work. To the best of my knowledge, no other theologian has focused attention so forcefully or so originally on the theological interpretation of contemporary secular society. Cox poses questions which no theologian concerned with our culture can readily ignore.

According to Cox, the rise of urban civilization and the collapse of traditional religion are the main hallmarks of our times. Cox contends that "the secular metropolis stands as both the pattern of our life together and the symbol of our view of the world" (p. 1). It has been made possible by the related processes of urbanization and secularization. The fruit of secularization and urbanization is technopolis, the evolving form of contemporary urban civilization. According to Cox, the relationships between men in technopolis tend to be functional and contractual in contrast to the emotionally overdetermined relationships which characterized the earlier and more primitive forms of social order he designates as the tribe and the town.

Few theologians have celebrated the anonymity and mobility of the secular city as enthusiastically as Cox. He makes the very telling point that in spite of the problems of technopolis few of us would return to the culture of the small town, with its seething hostilities, envies and built-in limitations to personal freedom. He is also very helpful in pointing out that urban life need not necessarily be dehumanized because of the absence of the I–Thou relationship, and he suggests the possibility of what he calls the I–You relation as typical within the anonymous metropolis. Such a relation may involve far less spontaneity and intimacy than the I-Thou relation. It does, however, offer the opportunity for the dignified meeting of persons who must maintain their distance because of the impersonal demands of city living. Cox's insight is a healthy antidote to those who bemoan the absence of genuine I–Thou relations but who fail to understand that there can be a decent alternative.

Cox is unsparing in his criticism of what he regards, I think mistakenly, as the antiurban bias of most important modern writers. He feels that their delineation of the problematics of the modern city has romantic elements of yearning to return to a dead past. It does not seem to have occurred to him that writers like Kafka, Proust, Joyce and Sartre understood the irreversibility of the processes which have created the modern city. They did not seek to return to an unavailable past, but to delineate the price in human terms we have paid and will continue to pay for the advantages of the modern world. One does not have to be wholeheartedly for or against the contemporary city. It is possible to cherish many of its advantages yet remain undeceived about the bitter price it frequently entails.

Perhaps the most theologically questionable aspect of Cox's enterprise is his enthusiastic embrace of the secular city and his identification of it with the Kingdom of God. Cox is too competent a theologian to be trapped into identifying the contemporary metropolis with the *realized* Kingdom. There are obviously too many negative aspects to it. He is amply safeguarded with an arsenal of categories such as "immature" and "primitive survivals" which he can conveniently append to unpleasant and degrading aspects of the secular city. He

relies heavily on the notion that the Kingdom is in the process of realizing itself in history. It is neither something that
has already occurred nor something which will finally occur
sometime in the future. It has been occurring at least since
the Christ event.

I must confess that I fail to find any meaningful content to
Cox's eschatology-in-process or his identification of elements
within the secular city with the Kingdom. I get the feeling
reading Cox, as I do reading Thomas J. J. Altizer, that I am
thrown into the oldest of all Judaeo-Christian debates—the
question of whether it can meaningfully be stated in any
sense that the Messiah has come. Even in the world of the
"death of God," the new Protestant theologians cannot
forego the good news of some order of Messianic fulfillment.
Like the Pharisees of old, I look in vain for any real evidence
of God's redemptive work as continuously manifest in the
world. Although Cox identifies Pharisaism with compulsive
attachment to a dead law, I think the real significance of
Pharisaism rests in its openness to the question of man's
relation to God and fellow man in a world in which eschatological yearning is a vain and futile illusion.

Apart from the age-old Judaeo-Christian debate on Messianism, an eschatology-in-process such as Cox's threatens
to become a specialized form of religious journalism in which
the eschatological interpreter picks and chooses those events
of which he approves as evidence of the Kingdom, while
relegating events he regards negatively as evidence of "im-
maturity" or "tribalism." Thus Cox strongly approves of Saul
Alinsky's Woodlawn experiment and interprets it as evidence
of the Kingdom. I do not know enough about Alinsky to form
a sound judgment, but I have heard some responsible men of
goodwill bitterly denounce both Alinsky and Woodlawn while
others have been equally unreserved in their praise. The
prophet's role is a hazardous one. Are we to interpret the
Kingdom in terms of today's newspaper reports or are we to
await the more balanced assessment of the historian writing
long after the fact? When and how do we really know that
the Kingdom is breaking in upon us?

It may be that Cox's conception of eschatology involves
the notion that everything that happens in history is part of

the process of the Kingdom realizing itself. This would be somewhat similar to Hegel's view, but Hegel understood that the final return of *Geist* unto itself could only be accomplished through all the negativities, crimes and tragedies of the historical process. I doubt that Cox would really be disposed to buy that package. It would involve seeing evidence of the Kingdom in such expressions of contemporary technopolis as Auschwitz, which was a highly rational, technopolitan factory for the manufacture of corpses, and the Negro urban ghetto. Cox has things too easy when he can identify those social phenomena of which he approves with the Kingdom while dismissing those he rejects as primitive survivals.

There is a deeper reason for Cox's dilemma. It is doubtful that a meaningful theology of history can be formulated at all unless one believes that some moment of *kairos* which has happened or will happen has the power to transform the conditions under which men experience their world. It is possible for the Christian, who believes that the coming of the Christ has made an actual, discernible difference, to have a theology of history. The Christian believer will, however, have to explain the apparent lack of empirical warrant for his assertions. It is equally possible for the traditional Jew to have a theology of history, viewing the story of humanity as a progression toward an as yet unrealized Messianic fulfillment. I doubt that Cox's indefinite, unspecified identification of the Kingdom with some aspects of technopolis will yield results. He wants the best of two somewhat incompatible worlds, that of the social scientist and that of the theologian. Cox must insist upon assigning superordinate meanings which they themselves do not yield to empirical events. The last thing social science can countenance is the kind of perjorative evaluations of modes of social encounter to be found on almost every page of *The Secular City*.

It is entirely possible to regard the modern metropolis simply as one of the many possible arrangements men have devised for securing the conditions and commodities necessary for the survival of its members. Such a view of technopolis is more in accord with contemporary anthropological and sociological insights than Cox's view, which uses theologically and emotionally loaded terms such as "Gospel" and "Law" to distinguish technopolis from societies which require a less rational technology but a more complex structure of myth and ritual. Other societies have employed alternative modes of social and cultural organization. None has succeeded entirely in meeting the biological and psychological needs of their members. Each has characteristic advantages and disadvantages. The Spanish peasant living in an authoritarian, impoverished, traditional nation is not necessarily worse off than the rootless, anxious, prosperous junior executive working for a large technopolitan corporation and living in the pleasant, well-to-do Shadyside district of Pittsburgh. There are many things the Spanish peasant has which the Pittsburgh executive needs: a sense of inner dignity, a secure knowledge of the rules of the game of life, a tragic sense of his place in society and in the order of things and, above all, a strong sense of personal and sexual identity. He may not live as long as the Pittsburgh executive. He certainly will have none of the American's comforts or his high mobility, but he will be far less likely to be beset with the emotional disturbances which are endemic among successful Americans.

Although Cox utilizes the language of psychoanalysis when it suits his purposes, he seems indifferent to an important analytic insight about the function of myth and ritual in religion, their capacity to objectify and dramatize the unconscious strivings of the individual in a significant social structure. Cox welcomes the advent of technopolis because of its use of a rational, pragmatic approach to the problems of life. He sees this structure as preferable to those societies which cope with the problems of life through the instrumentalities of myth, ritual and folk tradition. He is antitraditional in the extreme. The past is the trap from which men must extricate themselves; traditional societies are to technopolis as Law is to Gospel. According to Cox, most traditions are irrational reminders of the childhood of mankind. Those men who are free from the restraints of tradition and myth and who are capable of dealing with life in the most functional terms can be regarded as truly mature and fit for full adult citizenship in technopolis.

I am somewhat surprised at Cox's excessive concentration on the rational and conscious aspects of life, although such an overemphasis is by no means uncommon in Protestantism, as Paul Tillich has suggested in *The Protestant Era*.* Myth is more than prescientific explanation and ritual more than superstitious mumbo jumbo. If the insights of depth-psychology have any validity, myth must be seen as the attempt of a community to objectify and thus to deal with its deepest psychic and interpersonal dilemmas. Similarly, traditional ritual offers members of a community the opportunity to cope, both consciously and unconsciously, with the crises of life.

There are at least two over-all styles of religious life, one of which is moralistic, didactic, antiemotional and antiritualistic, while the other stresses the importance of ritual, tradition and emotional catharsis. I would like to call these two approaches Protestant and Catholic respectively. Cox's approach is severely Protestant. Were I a Christian, I would undoubtedly be Anglican or Roman Catholic. I believe that Protestantism's fundamental difficulty is that it has attempted to weaken or eliminate those elements in religion which permit us to deal with our emotions as we face the decisive crises of life. The chaste severity of the New England church reflects a certain icy chilliness; the florid expressiveness of Mediterranean baroque allows infinitely more emotion to enter religious experience. Is it really progress, as Cox seems to suggest, to exchange a religious life with a plenitude of emotional expressiveness for a desiccated rationalism which forces emotional response out of the sanctuary and into the marketplace?

The Protestant rejections of Mary and the sacrament of confession are two examples of the process of rationalization which Cox views so positively. It is possible to see both rejections as containing psychological difficulties from which Protestantism has never entirely extricated itself. By rejecting Mary, Protestantism lost any mythic way of coming to terms

* Paul Tillich, *The Protestant Era*, abridged (Chicago: The University of Chicago Press, 1957), p. xiv. "Protestants often are unaware of the numinous power inherent in genuine symbols. . . . They have replaced the great wealth of symbols appearing in the Christian tradition by rational concepts, moral laws and subjective emotions."

with the awesome, though terrible, realities of femininity and maternity. A myth was swept away, but an opportunity was lost for providing men with a religiocultural context in which their most archaic conflicts could be expressed and partly dealt with. The loss of the confessional left most Protestants, as Cox understands, without an effective instrumentality for dealing with their feelings of guilt. Since so great a proportion of our feelings of guilt are irrational and unconscious, the loss of mythic and ritual structures with which to manage them could not be balanced by a gain in conscious rational insight. It seems to me, as an outsider, that Cox's understanding of religion is provincially Protestant. I understand the inevitability of his Protestantism. I question his attempt to deal with other, equally valid religious options as if they were primitive, prescientific anticipations of his "mature," "free," "adult" approach. Hegel saw the history of philosophy as culminating in his own thought. He viewed every previous position as a *praeparatio evangelium* of his own. There is more than a little of the same kind of systematizing in Cox. Kierkegaard understood in opposition to Hegel that the experiences of unique, irreplaceable men could not be reduced to ontological categories. Neither can they be reduced to Cox's sociotheological categories.

Every society has its characteristic advantages and disabilities. The social scientist can describe the ways in which societies function. Nothing in his empirical or conceptual apparatus allows him to interpret what he finds in such theological categories as the realization of the Kingdom of God. When Cox attempts to introduce theological categories into his interpretation of historical or sociological phenomena, his assertions are either meaningless or arbitrary. If he wishes to assert that whatever has happened in history is an exemplification of the coming of the Kingdom, he has so relativized the category as to make it meaningless. If he means that only certain events express the realization of the Kingdom, he reduces the theology of history to his own special collection of likes and dislikes concealed under the rubric of categories such as "mature," "immature," "tribal," "ritualistic" and the like.

I should like to suggest another eschatology in place of

Cox's. Perhaps it is an antieschatology, for I believe that eschatology is a sickness with which man conceals from himself the tragic and ultimately hopeless character of his fate. There is only one Messiah who redeems us from the irony, the travail and the limitations of human existence. Surely he will come. He is the Angel of Death. Death is the true Messiah and the land of the dead the place of God's true Kingdom. Only in death are we redeemed from the vicissitudes of human existence. We enter God's Kingdom only when we enter His holy nothingness. Eschatology has absolutely no meaning in terms of earthly existence. I do not desire to enter God's Kingdom, because I prefer the problematics of finitude to their dissolution in the nothingness of eternity. No actual historical event can be identified with the coming of His Kingdom.

Father Andrew Greeley has asked (see pp. 101–108) whether the secular city pictured by Cox exists at all. He argues that the American metropolis offers little evidence of having evolved into the pragmatic, future-oriented community based upon function and contract which Cox describes. According to Father Greeley, religion and ethnicity seem to play ever larger roles in American cities. He cites the example of Chicago, which is divided into a host of religious and ethnic subgroups. These function as primary groups for many of the residents of technopolis. Most people enter the larger, technopolitan world only to fulfill specialized contractual relations. What Father Greeley writes of Chicago is also true of Pittsburgh and, I suspect, every other large American city. What appears to be a metropolitan community turns out to be a series of relatively small subcommunities separated by race, religion, national origin and economic circumstance.

There is devastating anonymity in the modern metropolis. One can be murdered in the streets without a flicker of concern from one's nearest neighbors. There is also a strong need for primary groups, the *gemeinschaft* of which Ferdinand Tönies has written. The proliferation of new churches and synagogues in the suburbs of America since World War II has perhaps been a partial response to that very need. Although didactic religious belief seems to have declined among virtually all American religious groups, there has been an unparalleled increase in the number and institutional strength of churches and synagogues. It is not surprising that Cox exhibits more than a little hostility to the organizational aspects of religious life in America. The institutional strength is in response to many of the primary needs which Cox would regard as archaic survivals.

Cox admits that there is a great deal of tribalism in American religion. He hopes for its eventual disappearance. In several places he quotes Paul's remark "There is neither Jew nor Greek . . ." as a scriptural warrant for technopolis. However, he does not complete the verse: "for ye are all one in Christ Jesus." For a non-Christian this is hardly the emblem of a secular society. It is the call of men to dissolve their previous religious and ethnic ties in order to create a new primary community. Cox may argue that this community is the forerunner of a truly secular society, but it hardly seems that way to non-Christians. A truly secular society would not require the kind of superordinate religious justification Cox offers in *The Secular City*. Furthermore, nothing so divides Jew and Christian as does the Law/Gospel dichotomy. That is not because Jews are compulsively bound to a meticulous system of legalistic trivia, but because Jews cannot conceive of a religious community or life without some degree of structure and discipline. We are not prepared to accept Cox's simplistic definition of what Law means to us. We have learned how to liberate ourselves from legalism while finding Law and freedom essentially compatible and interdependent.

This is not the place to debate the primitive, unhistorical view of Pharisaic Judaism which is implicit in Cox's categories. What must be stressed is the degree to which his categories are Protestant Christian. I fail to understand why one man's religious life must be regarded as tribal while Cox, Protestant to his very core, can insist that his theology has transcended the tribalisms and traditionalisms of the "earlier," "immature" religious postures. From the perspective of the non-Christian, Cox's theology of secularization is as deeply rooted in the Protestant past and even Protestant tribalism as any other religious option. I can only ask that he refrain from turning men of other religions into primitive anticipations of what he has become.

If anyone has any doubt about the pervasiveness of Protestant tribalism, E. Digby Baltzell's *The Protestant Establishment: Caste and Class in America* makes excellent reading. Baltzell's major concern is the extent to which the Protestant aristocracy which controls the major areas of economic and social power in America has become a caste based upon birth and race rather than an open class which admits men of ability regardless of background. The very areas of American life which Cox praises as being the most secular and pragmatic—the corporation and the university—are precisely the institutions in which Protestant tribalism is strongest. There is a very simple rule concerning eligibility for entrance into the managerial elite of the larger American corporations: one must be a WASP, a White Anglo-Saxon Protestant. This rule is observed with almost equal stringency in the administration of almost all non-Catholic American universities. Jews and Roman Catholics may hold distinguished academic teaching posts. They are almost never to be found directing or helping to direct the destinies of the universities at the administrative level. Baltzell's research suggests that the tendency of the Protestant community to form a caste within a larger American society has grown rather than diminished in recent years. I find it extremely difficult to take seriously Cox's contention that there is an evolving secular city. I find it even more difficult to take seriously Cox's view that the organization or corporation is the future-oriented, flexible, secularized institution Cox claims it is or is becoming. It may be that for Protestants, but for many others it remains a closed, tribal enclave.

I seriously question the way Cox demolishes his opponents. He does not argue their positions. He dissolves them into sociological or theological categories which exemplify progressions toward or regressions from his secular city. Thus philosophic existentialism and Paul Tillich's philosophy are dismissed as "expressions of the mourning period which began with the death of the God of metaphysical theism. . . ." (p. 80). The existentialists are "arcadian and antiurban" (p. 252) and of course there is "something immature about existentialism" (p. 253). Cox sees *Angst* as a category which

seems "increasingly irrelevant to the ethos of the new epoch"
(p. 80).

There is something Olympian in this approach. The existentialists were attempting to give an accurate picture of
their world as they experienced it. The best of them understood that no two men experience the world in quite the same
way. *Angst* is more than an increasingly irrelevant category.
It is a terrifying mode of encountering the reality that all life
hovers over a nothingness into which it will ultimately dissolve. As long as men are going to die, some will experience
the terrors of *Angst*. Paul Tillich's description of *Urangst* in
*The Courage to Be* offers insight into a primordial mode of
experiencing one's world rather than a cultural phenomenon
which will disappear in time.

Cox may not have experienced *Angst*. His may be a contemporary example of "the religion of healthy-mindedness"
described by William James. There is no reason why Cox
must experience *Angst*, but he might well take James' typology of "the sick soul" seriously. James did not dismiss "the
sick soul" as an outmoded survival. He understood that there
are a number of equally valid modes of religious experience.
He described them with insight and accuracy. He never reduced a religious or psychological experience to a primitive
expression of a particular era.

I wish Cox were right about *Angst*. Life would be a lot
easier. Cox's inability to appreciate the reality of *Angst* is, I
believe, symptomatic of a larger defect of vision. Cox offers
little evidence of possessing anything remotely like a tragic
sense of life. There is something very success-oriented about
his theology. He approves the mobility and anonymity of the
city, but says hardly enough about the hideous price the poor
have had to pay in rootlessness, disorientation and suffering
as a result of these phenomena. Anonymity and mobility can
be enormously helpful to successful, highly educated young
men who are part of what *Life* magazine recently called the
"take-over generation." They constitute an impossible burden
for the millions of Americans who lack the personal, social or
psychological resources with which to take advantage of the
new freedom. *Angst* may not be too great a problem for

young men who have succeeded in their chosen vocations beyond their expectations. It is natural for such young men to view life optimistically and to derive great satisfaction from the knowledge of their own competence. Unfortunately, they are exceptional even in our age of prosperity and advanced technology. For every person who can look back upon his life and say. "I'd do it the same way if I could do it over again," there are a hundred who have experienced a large measure of inner conflict, turmoil and defeat, no matter how outwardly successful they may appear. Few of them, few men of any condition, can look with equanimity upon old age or death. It is not likely that any society will reduce the level of realistic anxiety most men must endure.

Men do wonder where they come from, what is the meaning of life and what will be their ultimate destiny. From the time of the earliest attempts of archaic men to deal with the questions of origin and final end through their simple but compelling images of the Great Mother to the present day, what Paul Tillich called "ultimate concern" has been an awesome reality. "Ultimate concern" as a term may have been invented by Tillich, but the human reality to which it points is as old as religion itself. Paul Tillich has but barely departed from our midst. A new generation of theologians is arising, most of whom were his pupils. Let us not dismiss too readily or with undue haste those insights in his work which are of perennial significance and which may very well become a part of the classical inheritance of theology in the Western world.

Cox's inability to see the tragic dimension shows through in his interpretation of Albert Camus. According to Cox, Camus went "far beyond the anguished existentialism of many of his contemporaries" (p. 70). Camus did celebrate the joys of "the invincible summer" as Cox suggests, but he wrote with great lucidity of the price we pay for those joys. Few modern writers have celebrated the satisfactions of the flesh and of this world as fully as Camus in his marvelous essay "Summer in Algiers," yet this very essay describes with uncompromising clarity how those who live by the flesh have nothing but the flesh in the end. Death in Algiers was devoid of all consolation. For Camus the invincible summer was inevitably followed by the cold of autumn and winter. Of all the evils let loose from Pandora's box, Camus tells us, the worst was hope. Camus is undeceived about life. His vision is ennobling but unreservedly tragic. Camus was not, as Cox suggests, an atheistic Christian. He was a Mediterranean pagan. He lived in the realm of the Great Goddess and all of his work can be seen as a latter-day expression of her religion. In his essay "Helen's Exile," as well as in the concluding part of *The Rebel*, Camus rejects the very Messianism which permeates Cox's work.

It is not true as Cox suggests that Camus rejected God primarily because He contradicts human freedom. It is true of Sartre and Nietzsche but not of Camus. The God whom Camus rejects is the very God whom Cox affirms, the biblical God of history. In *The Plague*, Camus utilizes the character of Father Paneloux to illustrate the difficulty of believing in the God of history in the twentieth century. The plague which besets Oran in the novel is Camus' symbol for the irrational human and natural evils which have confronted men in our times. The varying responses of Camus' characters to the plague represent the ways in which men have reacted to the disasters of the twentieth century, especially World War II and the death camps. The most important reactions are those of Father Paneloux and Dr. Rieu. Camus utilizes a sermon by Father Paneloux to illustrate the classical Judaeo-Christian reaction to the terrible fact of disaster. Because Father Paneloux believes God to be the omnipotent Lord of history, he must see the plague as an expression of God's punitive retribution. He interprets the disaster, as the prophets and teachers of Israel and the theologians of the church have interpreted similar disasters for millennia, as God's chastisement of a sinful world. He must interpret the plague in this way or accept an element of absurdity and mystery in the order of things for which he is psychologically unprepared. He lacks the courage of the absurd. "Men have sinned, God has punished. Repent and God will heal!" is the essence of his message.

Father Paneloux's theology of history breaks down as he watches a small boy die horribly of the plague. According to his theology, the child must be a sinner, but every human instinct within the priest rejects this. In the presence of the real suffering and death of a child, Father Paneloux's whole attempt to construct a theological interpretation of history disintegrates. Paneloux dies shortly thereafter, not of the plague but of the loss of his world. What Camus demonstrates is that, if there is a God of history, the measure of punishment he metes out to men is totally incommensurate with their actual guilt. The God of history is incompatible with human dignity as well as human freedom.

Cox insists that "God does reveal His name in history, through the clash of historical forces and the faithful efforts of a people to respond to his call" (p. 266). Were Cox to take Camus seriously, he would understand how profoundly untenable this position is. If there is a God of history, He is the ultimate author of Auschwitz. I am willing to believe in God the Holy Nothingness Who is our source and our final destiny, but never again in a God of history. Cox sees the action of the God of history in technopolis. If there is such a God, He has also manifested Himself in Auschwitz. Few ideas in Jewish religious thought have been more decisively mistaken, in spite of their deep psychological roots, than the terrible belief that God acts meaningfully in history. When the existentialists claim that they fail to find meaning and purpose in the order of things, they do not mean, as Cox seems to suggest, that *everything* is meaningless and purposeless. No serious existentialist ever claimed this. Sartre, for example, insists that human existence is inseparable from the reality of *praxis,* by which he means any meaningful labor toward an end or a goal.* What the existentialists do mean is that there is no *ultimate* meaning to existence. They call upon men to create with lucidity their own private meanings and purposes in the knowledge that no power in the cosmos will deliberately sustain or validate them.

Those who accept the existentialist rejection of meaning in history do so largely because they prefer an absurd cosmos to one in which every significant instance of human suffering must be interpreted as the chastisement visited upon guilty humanity by an omnipotent and punitive God.

Cox is deeply influenced by Dietrich Bonhoeffer's question

* Jean Paul Sartre, *Critique de la raison dialectique* (Paris: Gallimard, 1960), pp. 165ff.

of April 30, 1944: "How do we speak of God without religion?" As I have suggested at the beginning of this essay, I
believe the real question should not be how we speak of God
without religion but how we speak of religion in the time of
"the death of God." Even Cox admits that the names men
have constructed for God are somehow without meaning in
our time and that we experience what he regards as God's
absence or eclipse. What the death-of-God theologians depict
is an indubitable cultural fact in our times: God is totally
unavailable as a source of meaning or value. There is no
vertical transcendence. Our problem is not how we shall
think of God in a secular way. It is how men can best share
the decisive crises of life, given the cold, unfeeling, indifferent
cosmos that surrounds us and given the fact that God the
Holy Nothingness offers us only dissolution and death as the
way out of the dilemmas of earthly existence.

It is in this situation that the traditional church and synagogue are most meaningful. We need the religious institution
—the church for Christians and the synagogue for Jews—
precisely because the human condition is unredeemed in the
present and ultimately hopeless in what lies beyond the existential horizon. The prophetic role of religion as a social
catalyst stressed by Cox is quite secondary. Religion cannot
be indifferent to social justice but neither can its major task
be equated with its pursuit. The primary role of religion is
priestly. If offers men a ritual and mythic structure in which
the abiding realities of life and death can be shared. As long
as men are born, pass through the crises of transition in life,
experience guilt, fail, as fail they must, grow old and die,
traditional churches and synagogues will be irreplaceable institutions. It is very difficult for any sensitive intellectual to
feel entirely at home in the middle-class churches or synagogues of suburban America. Nevertheless, we ought not to
permit our own discomfort to obscure from us the abiding
value of these institutions.

Few men who studied under Paul Tillich could have been
anything but deeply moved by the news of his death. I
learned of his passing while visiting Warsaw, Poland. I had
just returned from visiting the site of the Warsaw ghetto for
the first time. Somehow, there was something appropriate in

hearing the sad news in that place. An important part of Tillich's greatness was his ability to endow with theological meaning the universal dissolution in two world wars of the old certainties of European civilization. Tillich had known the stability which preceded the breakdown. He had the courage to confront the breakdown and discern within it possibilities of theological renewal.

My sadness was tempered by the knowledge that Tillich's work was, insofar as any man's can be, completed. He had spoken for and to his time, but we have moved beyond that time. I could not help but wonder as I thought about his passing what would be the issues and who would be the men to interpret them in the age of the evolving civilization which looms before us. No theologian could speak effectively to his time during the first half of the twentieth century unless he were deeply cognizant of the terrible facts of the breakdown and its human meaning. The possibility of the renewal of catastrophe has not departed but, hopefully, catastrophe will not be our problem in the foreseeable future. Our problems will be those of a mass, urban civilization in an overpopulated world. The new theological sensitivity cannot be indifferent to social structure or what it does to men. Cox's importance as a theologian resides in the fact that he has had the courage and the insight to face many of the most important problems which must dominate theological discussion in the period immediately before us. *The Secular City* also affords a partial answer to the question "Who are the men who will come after Tillich?" Cox is one of them and American theology will be enriched for many years by his brilliance.

Nevertheless, as I read his work, I found myself saying to him:

"Come down from Olympus, Harvey. Stop labeling ways of life foreign to your free-church background in categories that deprecate their unique relevance. There are many mansions. . . . Living traditions and communities cannot be reduced to abstract categories. Must we go through the debate of Kierkegaard and Hegel all over again?"

# CHAPTER 2

# A Little Bit of a Revolution?

*Steven S. Schwarzschild*

John Cogley has described Vatican Council II as the advance of the Ror an Catholic Church into the seventeenth century. Paul Van Buren, after he has finished being very shocking, favors all the virtues of orthodox theology and the Boy Scout Code. Harvey Cox proclaims that the pragmatic hero of his secularized Gospel is John F. Kennedy. I suppose we ought to be grateful for little favors: it could have been Richard Nixon—and in the past it often was. But we also have to realize that these favors are, indeed, little. And to use such grandiloquent phrases as "a theology of revolution" is at best pretentious. Real revolutionaries, in Afro-Asia, Warsaw, and Berkeley will, optimally, shrug their shoulders. Which Kennedy is Cox talking about? The Kennedy of the Bay of Pigs, the hereditary prince of a ruthless and opportunistic political family-empire, the advocate of rabidly racist Federal judges, and the patron of the arts whose idea of culture is *Camelot?*

But our argument is not primarily political. It is essentially theological. Cox, like so many other contemporary Christian theological "radicals"—including the "God-is-dead" theologians—is paying the price of having to be the antithesis of a meretricious thesis. The thesis of historical Christianity has been "otherworldliness." This has now become, if it was not always, irrelevant. The "radicals" are right in wanting to regain relevance; against the earlier otherworldliness they, therefore, pit their worldliness. Their technical term for worldliness is "secularity"; a philosophical term for it is "immanentism."

145

These "radical" theologians are, however, merely perpetuating the ancient error which they think they are combating. The old metaphysic said in effect: God is outside of this world; therefore, let the world be as it is. The new immanentism is saying in effect: the world is God; therefore, let the world become as it will.

This is an improvement. At least some possibility of change is envisioned. Thus, Cox speaks of the church as the avant-garde of God's Kingdom, and he realizes that the Kingdom is always ahead of where the world is and demands that the latter catch up with it. But he is taking, as I say, a very small step. The Kingdom is always only one little step ahead of the world, never two steps, and certainly not an infinite distance—and the direction which the Kingdom urges is always the one in which the world is going already. To call "revolution" what is really an extremely gradual development in a direction already determined by the present situation is to misuse the English language. The world is still essentially being left where it is, or let go where it is going (*sich realisierende Eschatologie*). The proper word for this is "conservatism."

The reason for this built-in Christian conservatism is, as Cox is perfectly aware, the doctrine of the Incarnation. What this doctrine minimally means is that at least one person, at one time and in one place, has been divine. That is to say, the world as it now is, and indeed as it once was, has been at least partly redeemed—and therefore the whole world as it now is is in principle capable of redemption. Cox's only argument with the reactionaries is that they think the entire world is already completely redeemed. The issue between them is one of degree, not of principle.

*Corruptio optimi pessima.* Even though Cox is fully aware of the need for "Hebraizing" the pagan metaphysics of classic Christian theology, I fear that he is caught up in something that he surely hates profoundly: the ideological bias of cultural, ethnic, political, and religious egocentrism—Christian egocentrism. The catalogue of Cox's fantastic historical falsifications and profound misunderstandings of Judaism, "Pharisaic Judaism," includes legalistic psychoneurosis, sexual hypocrisy, tribal chauvinism, demonism, etc.

What is it about his theology that forces him into this position, and in what relationship does this stand to his fundamental conservatism?

Judaism is not immanentist. It is not solely transcendentalist either, because that would imply that God has no relationship to the world. Perhaps the best way to put it is that the God of Israel is totally concerned with the world precisely because He is entirely beyond it. Among other things, this means that the Kingdom is not here in any fashion and to any degree; the Messiah has not yet arrived. Cox is entirely right when he says that genuine biblical faith is truly revolutionary: it demands the complete overthrow of the present world because this world is totally different from what God wants it to be. The Law of Revelation is the exact opposite of what Cox—in his perhaps most objectionably anti-Judaic misrepresentation—defines it as being; it is not the dead hand of past social institutions but the commands of the future Kingdom upon present man.

One specific example: A Marxist would be wryly amused by Cox's squirmings on the question of private property. Cox states correctly and with apparent sympathy that, according to Marxist doctrine, only a rearrangement of property relations can correct the "false consciousness" of an immoral culture. That would be a pretty daring and genuinely revolutionary theologumenon. Cox does not have such daring and quickly hides behind such spiritualistic categories as "message," "service," and "fellowship." In activist circles these pretty phrases are recognized as soft soap. You do not change the basic realities of our society with them—indeed, they are evidence that you do not really want to.

On the other hand, Cox quotes Luke 4:18f. I claim no competence as a New Testament theologian, but it seems perfectly clear to me that, if Jesus there spoke as a Jew, he was actually doing what Jeremiah had done before him in besieged Jerusalem—demanding the fulfillment of the Levitical law (!) of the Sabbath and of the Sabbatical and Jubilee years. Never mind such fancy terms as *"kerygma," "dia-*

*konia*," and *"koinonia"*—return the land to the proprietorship of the sanctified community! This is real, even as Cox correctly recognizes that the Negro is not primarily concerned with whether you love him but with a job, a decent home, a doctor, a teacher for his children, and an effective vote. Furthermore, in Judaism the Sabbath law (and, indeed, the law of "the eternal Sabbath," which is the Messianic Kingdom) long ago broke the employment-income nexus not only in theory but also in practice. (See my "The Necessity of the Lone Man," *Fellowship*, May, 1965.)

The doctrine of the Incarnation, which says that redemption already exists in this world, has always tempted Christians to make their peace with whatever this world has been at any given time. Under the Nazis it called itself "German Christianity." Now Cox sympathizes with the Christians behind "the Iron Curtain" who give their political loyalty to the Communist states while retaining their ideological aloofness. I agree with him that Karl Barth's positive though critical stance toward Communism (unblemished as it is, on the whole, by previous political betrayals) is preferable to Bishop Dibelius' sacred crusade against Marxist atheism (laden down, as *it* is, with a history of collaboration with German archconservative nationalism and postwar apologetics). But one has reason to think that Cox's understanding for Communist Christians is due not to an appreciation of the ethical difference between Nazism and Communism but to the fact that Communism in fact exists at the present historical juncture—and, incarnationally, pantheistically, "all that is is rational." After all, the "organization man" also is—whatever is is "the wave of the future" (p. 6)—and thus Cox welcomes the organization man as the new Christian.

The only thing that he objects to in the organization is that it is not sufficiently organizational: there are still tribal or familial elements left in the bureaucracy. He holds that the completion of the organization in economic life will give us a chance for what Goethe called *"Wahlverwandschaften,"* i.e., the opportunity to chose our own spiritual family and friends. (Compare this to what Benjamin F. Payton rightly analyzes

as the causal relationship between Negro misery in the North
and the megalopolis which Cox so welcomes: "New Trends
in Civil Rights," *Christianity and Crisis*, Dec. 13, 1965.)
Knowing what we do about the dynamics of modern organization and what Cox himself alludes to as its imperfections, it
is very difficult, if not impossible, to avoid the conclusion that
the organization by its very nature will usurp the place and
the power of the sanctified family. In my last community the
General Electric Company was well-known for shifting its
executive personnel around the country sufficiently often so
that they and their families would end up having only one
community, the organization, its country clubs and other
appurtenances. In my present community the workers at Mc-
Donnell Aircraft are out on strike as I write. This is the first
such episode in decades, and it is the more remarkable in that
no financial issues divide the parties; but Mr. McDonnell
frequently gives mawkish speeches over the plant loudspeaker
system in which he addresses everybody as a "teammate" and
a member of one big, happy family of equals.

Cox suggests that Buber's distinction between I–Thou and
I–It relationships ought to be supplemented with the category
of I–You relationships, *i.e.*, limitedly, functionally personal
relations in the secular city. Buber would have regarded this
as a *contradictio in adjecto:* functional relations are the precise opposite of personal relations.

Be that as it may, in his climactic last, theological chapter,
Cox applies this I–You category to God Himself. He realizes,
of course, that a completely immanent God can hardly be a
God of revolution. God has to be at least somewhat outside
of what is, in order to open the way for what is not yet. But
since Cox is less interested in revolution than in gradual
change along lines which have already been projected, a God
is needed who is a tiny little bit transcendent. And that is
precisely the God he gives us. It is a God with whom men do
not have an I–Thou but an I–You relationship. He defines
this not so much as confrontation but as "alongsidedness"
and compares it to the way men work together as equals on a
modern technical team.

At this point the tendentious falsehood of Cox's biblical

theology needs to be explicated. Cox begins by claiming that
the YHWH of the Bible has usually been translated as *deus,
theos,* or God. This is simply false. The usual translation of
YHWH has in fact been *kyrios, dominus,* or Lord. The point
is important, because Cox rightly insists that God ought to be
a name, not a word of meaning. *Deus* is a generic term, not a
name, corresponding more to the Hebrew *'elohim.* By means
of this error Cox degrades the biblical God into the class of
ancient deities—in the best tradition of German anti-Semitic
"scholarship." Thus he goes on to the statement "Tribal man
experienced God as one of the 'gods.' The Old Testament,
incorporating elements of this tribal mentality, is in no sense
'monotheistic.' Yahweh is the ruler of the gods" (p. 245).
Now, this is either so incredibly and frightfully subtle that it
completely escapes my understanding, or it is so horrible that
no sophomore could get away with it. I have gone through all
the usual claptrap of modern biblical scholarship, but at its
very worst I have never before seen even an intimation of this
claim. The God of all of the Bible is really "in no sense"
monotheistic?—Cox ends by translating the famous theo-
phanic pronouncement in Exodus 3:14 as "I will do what I
will do." Perhaps Professor Cox's Hebrew is better than mine
and everybody else's, but, whatever divergencies of view on
this *crux interpretationem* may exist, this is an entirely new
version. Where *do* our self-proclaimed scientific academicians
get the absolute confidence of their willfulness?

Why then does Cox propound such nonsense? Because he
has to justify the thesis that the God of the Bible is the God
of Christianity, and that He is a little bit transcendent—but
not too much. (I do not wish to sound either blasphemous or
disrespectful, but I am irrepressibly reminded of the girl who
was "a little bit pregnant.") The God of the Hebrew Bible,
therefore, has to be tribalized, and the God of Christianity
has to be de-immanentized in just the right measure.

But this God is "transcendent" in a very peculiar way (if I
understand Cox here correctly). In the first place, Cox uses
the term "hidden God" as synonymous with "transcendent
God"—but that is not common usage. To be sure, a transcendent God is perforce always somewhat hidden, but when

we speak nowadays of the hiddenness of God we mean that even the revealed part of God (*en façon de parler*) is hiding itself in our time—and this is the agony of our experience. In any event, both the transcendence and the hiddenness in Cox's definition turn out to be virtually synonymous with His immanence: "He hides Himself in the stable of human history" (p. 258)—and "Thus we meet God at those places in life where we come up against that which is not pliable and disposable, at those hard edges where we are both stopped and challenged to move ahead. God meets us as the transcendent, at those aspects of our experience which can never be transmuted into extensions of ourselves. He meets us in the wholly other" (p. 262).

Now, if this means anything it is that the transcendence of God is identical with the stubbornness of historical (and perhaps also natural) facticities. Here the chastened liberal seems to be saying that men cannot, after all, shape the world completely according to their own wishes. This is a useful insight—but it surely is not divine transcendence. It is, again, the power of the immanent. Divine transcendence means, among other things, that nature and history, however ultimately unmalleable by human hands, are at least in creation and in the *eschaton* subject to God's free disposition. Thus it is perfectly consistent for Cox to express some vestigial agreement with the "God-is-dead" theologians; though he argues against Van Buren's explicit immanentism, his own transcendentalism turns out to be only verbally different. (Though he has been sharply condemned for it, I think David Little's criticism in "The Social Gospel Revisited" [see pp. 69–74] comes as close to recognizing this as the real problem as any.)

One must try to be fair to this form of secularism. These current Protestant thinkers are honestly attempting to do something very worthwhile and important. They realize that Western, bourgeois culture is moribund, if not dead—that its gods have commonly been idols—and that religion, if it is to mean anything, has to be relevant to the world. Religion has to be ethical and political. On this we can all agree. It is a long overdue "Judaization" of Christianity. But these thinkers are in error in believing that this goal can be reached through an "immanentization" of God. Where God is dead, man also dies. Ethics means that there are values and standards beyond man. Nietzsche and Dostoevsky understood better than the theologians that when God has died everything becomes possible. If we are lucky, the atheists, like Marx and Camus, will create their own values, which, largely, coincide with those of authentic biblical religion. But if we are unlucky—and that is at least equally possible—the atheists, like de Sade, Alfred Rosenberg, Stalin, etc., will create ethical monstrosities. And if we end up between the two, in a world without either given or self-created values, the anomie, rootlessness, and indifferentism of the modern world will ensue.

There is another danger in the exhaustively politicized, immanentized God which these well-intentioned new ethicists overlook. This is a danger to religion—better, to faith. Worried about the relevance of religion, they feel it has to be politicized. The truly secular man, however, will use Occam's razor: I can, and many do, engage committedly in politics without faith; why then should I need faith? The truly religious man, on the other hand, is bound to arrive at the point, at one time and another, when "the world is too much with" him. It is exhilarating to watch young Americans in their new-found political enthusiasm—but old Jews, old Asians, and old Europeans have had so very much of politics! They know that there is a dimension of human existence which lies outside of politics and which makes human existence human. Without that dimension also politics will, in the end, be unbearable. (This is something that Kierkegaard and some of the existentialists whom Cox so abhors understand.)

God is—at least also—the God of this unpolitical dimension. This is not mysticism. It is humanism; it makes the human being human. It is also humanism in a very political, in an unpolitically political sense: Cox accepts Theobald's view of the future of cybernetic society; but when work will have become supererogatory, so will politics. Politics is, after all, as "we good Marxists" know, a function of economics. And that is where the transcendent God, Who also transcends

although He is in politics, comes into His own—Psalms
65:2: "To Thee silence is praise." (See C. C. West, "What It
Means to Be Secular," see p. 59: "There are times in the life
of the secular city and in the course of a revolution when
one is called not to be active but passive, not to talk but to
listen . . .")

Another important criticism must be leveled at the pro-
posed concept of an I–You relationship. The Jewish theologian E. Berkovits has rightly observed that the I–Thou and
I–It dichotomy leaves little room for a very special human
relationship which is enshrined in the Bible and the covenantal life, the I–We relationship. To such a critique Cox
does not, and cannot, rise. The social, more-than-individual
dimension of human existence has always lain outside the
universe of normative Christian discourse. Despite his political interests, Cox remains within this historic Christian limit,
by welcoming the atomization of the sanctified family by
modern, mobile technology.

Cox's section on the organization man turns one's mind to
the *kibbutzim,* on which Buber exerted great intellectual and
moral influence. Whatever the theoretical limitations of the
I–Thou concept, in practice Buber was an utopian socialist.
The *kibbutzim* try very hard to humanize modern social organization and economics; they abhor the organization
man—and it seems that lots of people in Africa and Asia,
and Christian utopians (whom Cox undoubtedly regards as
well-meaning atavists), are eager to learn from them. We are
back with the law of the Sabbatical year: the *kibbutzim* do
not even own their own land—it belongs to the community as
a whole. The religious *kibbutzim* are wrestling this very year
with the technicalities (I believe the Christian term for this is
"casuistry," and *Time* magazine has headlines about "Shmit-
tah and Sham") of having to let the land lie fallow for
God.

The theological principle in all this, I submit, is that only
radical transcendentalism, in the Jewish sense, and devout
concern with divine law can lead to an authentic revolutionary stance in the modern world. God is beyond the world,

not in it—and so is His Kingdom. The man of believing action feels under the ineluctable command to understand and to carry out the law which is to bring about the total revolution from "this world" to "the world-to-come." The Kingdom is a total, ultimate, unified vision; and it is, therefore, conducive to total, ultimate, and unified Messianic action. But of such total demands the men of little revolutions —not so much "of little faith"—are afraid, and their fear takes the form of a barbaric misreading of the (Hebrew) Bible. Christians are still shrinking from the imperatives of the law and in its stead put their faith in the present.

Let it be clear: The man of believing action is not laboring under the idolatrous illusion that he is bringing about the Kingdom; he is only trying to do God's will, so that He may, in His grace, bring it about. This unified vision cannot deteriorate into utopian totalitarianism (as Reinhold Niebuhr has made us constantly, bogeyman-like, worry), because the action program always knows itself to be human—and, therefore, under the judgment and in the need of divine consummation. But this man is also not engaging in any hand-to-mouth "pragmatic" meliorism. He knows that there will always be enough politicians around to compromise between the stand-pat reactionaries who proclaim that their world is the Kingdom of Heaven and his own genuinely eschatological demands. Harvey Cox's "lib-labism" will do in a pinch. But without religious or atheistic "extremists" the politicians would make their compromises far more to the "right."

To revert finally to my Jewish apologetic argument: This is a theology of the revolutionary, divine law. It may still strike some as casuistic and legalistic. I wonder whether there is a revolutionary on earth who would not prefer it to Cox's theology of punctuation marks (he calls it "the grammar of the Gospel"); for Cox, the Kingdom of God resides in the semi-colon of Mark 1:15 (p. 116)! Speaking of casuistry, my edition of the King James version has no semicolon there. Did the Septuagint? Or did divine revelation come only with the RSV?

I suppose I sound angry. To tell the truth, I am angry.

Once the bandwagon has begun to roll, Christian theologians persist in arrogating to themselves, or to Christianity, the titles of everything that Divine Revelation at Sinai, in Bible and Talmud, lays down to Jews—everything that conscientious Jews have worked hard through the centuries to enact in their personal and social lives—everything that Christian civilization with all its power has consistently tried to frustrate and everything that Christian and Jewish heretics have made operative in modern times. This is the more provoking as these same Christian theologians at the same time perpetuate the vicious myths of Jewish tribalism, *Werkheiligkeit,* and vengeful justice. I can put this more anecdotally: I like a record of folk songs by the Weavers which was recorded live at a Christmas night concert in New York; on it they sing a medley of the Hebrew song "Shalom chaverim" ("Peace, comrades") and a Christmas carol. Normally I would dislike intensely such eclecticism. In this case I find myself liking it for two reasons: I know that the crowds present at this concert "voted with their feet" by absenting themselves from midnight church services; and I know that, though the religious eclecticism may be shoddy, the social passion is genuine.

Let this bitter complaint be a contribution to honest "dialogue" as well as to a renewed understanding of the authentic revolutionary import of biblical actions of faith.

# CHAPTER 3

# Reflections on the Problem of Speaking of God

## Claude Welch

The whole argument of *The Secular City,* Harvey Cox
affirms at several points, depends on resolving the problem
posed in the final chapter: "To Speak of God in a Secular
Fashion." It is this problem which I want to approach, with
close attention to Cox's way of posing it. In one sense, the
affirmation just cited does not seem to me true. It is not clear,
for example, that the social analysis or indeed the ethical
prescription depends at all upon the particular kind of proposals Cox makes in his concluding discussion or upon certain of the positions taken earlier. Specifically, one could
justify the same refreshing stance toward the urban world
without at all being committed to Cox's kind of Christo-
centrism. One might also want to argue that the grateful
acceptance of the blessings of the city can be grounded even
better in a doctrine of creation than in a *sich realisierende*
eschatology. But in another sense, even more important,
everything does hang on the last chapter. Cox assumes that
Christian faith is possible and that it is possible to speak out
of such context in and to the world, and specifically to speak
of God's action. Thus it is indispensable that God-talk be
made intelligible. The whole appeal to the "biblical perspective" is utterly fruitless, indeed nothing more than a return to
a biblical ghetto, unless we can be satisfied that we mean
something when we talk about man's responding to God's
action.

Cox, it is evident, really means for us to speak of God. He
is not at all a "death-of-God" theologian. As he puts it most
sharply, ". . . despite . . . all the palaver about the terms

'existence' and 'being' and all the sophisticated in-group bickering about nonobjectifying language . . . there remains an indissoluble question after all the conceptualizations have been clarified . . . is man alone in the universe or not?" Again, "If man cannot speak of God in the secular city, then all we have said about secularization as the work of God for man is nonsense and the whole thesis of this book is erroneous" (pp. 241, 242).

Now let us grant fully that Cox does not intend to present us with a closed view or final statement, that he is genuinely posing a problem and looking for a way. His suggestions are thus open-ended. But as soon as we begin to look at Cox's particular proposals we have difficulties of several sorts, involving both the statement of why it is hard for secular man to speak about God and the pattern of speaking that Cox offers.

On the former count there is Cox's unfortunate tendency to make a systematic argument out of a historical sketch; viz. the account of development from "tribal" to "town" to "technopolitan" culture. However interesting this analysis may be as an attempt at periodization, it becomes treacherous and finally unfair as an argument—treacherous because for this to bear weight as an argument the development must be shown to have the character of historical necessity (thus the argumentative force is loaded into the description at the outset); unfair because substantive disagreements tend to be countered by relegating the opponent to a prior stage in historical development. A critical issue for our present discussion is why metaphysical or ontological language about God belongs to a tribal rather than an urban stage of existence. In speaking of this question, Cox lumps together strange bedfellows: the presumed antithesis of Greek and Hebrew modes of thought (a once popular but now severely questioned notion); a commonsense pragmatism that results from our finding an increasing number of aspects of life under our own control, thus with less and less place for a "special" divine action at the edges of existence; and the criticism of the "metaphysical" by Heidegger and by analytical philosophy (critiques that again have relatively little to do with each other). Even were it possible to show that such diverse elements converge to support a common modern mood, the description of that could hardly be substituted for systematic argument.

Cox's own approach to a positive statement begins with a word from Bonhoeffer to the effect that we do not properly speak "about" God but rather "name" God. At once an ambiguity emerges (and it is also present in the text from which Cox quotes). To speak of naming God rather than talking about Him can mean simply that religious language (if we may use the term without all the special and often ill-understood meanings that Bonhoeffer himself attached to the word "religious") is existential language; that is, significant talk "of" God is talk in which we are ourselves vitally involved. The theological task is thus rooted in "naming" as an act of confessing God, not in a neutral, speculative sort of question. But "naming" here may also suggest that "giving a name" to God can be a substitute for interpretation or can be an all-sufficient mode of denotation and identification. The latter meaning of "naming" certainly cannot be defended simply on the basis of the former, nor is it clear which Cox has in mind.

Closely related is Cox's failure to distinguish clearly between the confessing of faith and theological articulation. He speaks of the "theological question" as making us "answer for ourselves whether the God of the Bible is real or just a rich and imaginative way man has fashioned to talk about himself. No amount of verbal clarification can set this disagreement aside. In the last analysis it is not a matter of clear thinking at all but a matter of personal decision. Luther was right: deciding on this question is a matter which, like dying, every man must do for himself" (p. 243). But this kind of talk simply confuses the decision of faith with the theological task; the latter is precisely a verbal clarification and critical reflection that may presuppose a decision of faith but seeks to articulate it in intelligible form. Thus to speak of "naming God" may well direct us to the right starting place and indeed, as perhaps it does for Cox, to a larger view of what "speaking of God" means, but it certainly cannot be any

substitute for the theological articulation that seeks to explain
that to which faith is understood to be a response or decision.

Something of the same confusion seems to be present in
Cox's distinction between speaking of God as a "sociological
problem," as a "political issue," and as a "theological question." The first of these categories comprises an odd mixture
of (1) the familiar recognition that all our language is culturally conditioned; (2) a thoroughly question-begging em-
ployment of the tribal, town, technopolitan distinction, with a
quite forced assignment of various conceptions of "God" to
the earlier epochs (and since when would Saint Thomas have
been willing to speak of "God as a part of one unified structure including both God and man"?); and (3) some poignant
observations on the problems of communication resulting
from our various socially conditioned contexts for understanding. The only real specification of the "sociological"
problem comes at the point of the proposal "to speak about
God without a metaphysical system," but this is precisely
something that must be argued out as a theological question
and certainly cannot be justified simply by reference to the
sociology of knowledge. No substantive proposal is in fact
here made by Cox, only the formal call to "alter the social
context" for speaking of God and "to refuse to play out the
cultural roles which trivialize whatever the speaker says"(p.
248).

The discussion of "speaking of God as a political issue"
presents at first blush another odd contrast. Political action as
a way of speaking of God or of testimony to God is posed as
"an alternative" to metaphysical, premetaphysical (Heidegger
and Ott), and existentialist ways of speaking of God. I happen to concur with some of Cox's judgments about the efforts
of Heidegger and Ott, though he is wrong in suggesting that
they want to return to a kind of primitive mythical thinking,
and also with some of his critique of the claims existentialism
makes to speak for all modern men. Furthermore, one can
hardly fault Cox for insisting upon action—specifically, political action—as a mode of testimony to God. This is certainly
not new, though it may need to be said again and again. But

by what logic does it follow from this that "in secular society politics does what metaphysics once did" (p. 254). Granted that Christian reflection must focus on "the life and death issues of the secular metropolis. It must be reflection on how to come to political terms with the emergent technical reality which engulfs us" (*Ibid.*). But how does it follow that we have a "political" mode of theology that can and must *replace* metaphysical theology?

The answer to this question is presumably to be found in Cox's definition of what metaphysics once did. Specifically, it brought "unity and meaning to human life and thought" (*Ibid.*). But no overarching intellectual framework is available for unifying our world of truth and life; our world is rather "functionally unified by bringing disparate specialities to bear on the concrete political perplexities . . ." (*Ibid.*). Thus a political theology (or theological politics?) is one that will genuinely communicate to "urban-secular man." Thus it can be asserted that "politics is the language of evangelism." But if this is to say more than that the style of life in obedience and love, in the assisting of man to be truly human, is the most effective testimony to the truth of Christian faith, if it is to say that political theology is in fact a mode of statement of theology and thus an alternative to premetaphysical or metaphysical or existentialist theologies, then there must be some clear basis for this particular political theology's conception of "the responsible, adult agent, the fully post town and post tribal man God expects him to be today" (p. 255). If the meeting place with modern man is political, *i.e.*, if this is the place where unity and meaning are brought to his life, it still remains essential to show what are the distinctive characteristics of this peculiar Christian political theology. Yet throughout this discussion Cox seems to slip back into more ordinary senses of the assertion that the action of love is the best language of evangelism. He does not in fact show us how a political theology is able to do what metaphysics once did, but rather seems to be suggesting that what metaphysical theology once did can no longer be done, and that a political theology can do something different. Political theology at least does not do the specifically "theological" task.

So it is that Cox finally comes around to the "question" properly called theological and recognizes that important decisions must be made about "talking" about God. It will not do, he says, for God "to be identified with some particular quality in man or in human reciprocity" (pp. 259 f.), any more than for God to be considered only as an object of speculation or curiosity. On a Christian view, man is responsible and accountable to that which is not man. There is a real transcendence to be apprehended.

But where do we go from here? Essentially Cox suggests two kinds of considerations. The first is an appeal to the biblical doctrine of God's hiddenness. Here Cox rightly insists on the basic distinction between God's hiddenness and any simple absence of God or plain nontheism. Further, he rightly understands that God's hiddenness and His disclosure are not mutually exclusive but rather correlative concepts, that God's hiddenness is His freedom to be present without being available for coercion or manipulation. But at the same time Cox leaves us simply with the paradox that God "does not 'appear' but shows man that He acts, in His hiddenness, in human history" (p. 258). What does such a "showing" mean and what is shown? To that no clear answer is given.

Cox does go on to affirm that "the difference between men of biblical faith and serious nontheists is not that we do not encounter the same reality. The difference is that we give the reality a different *name,* and in naming it differently, we differ seriously in the way we respond" (p. 260). The implications of this are not much pursued, except in that the problem of the "transcendent" is at once taken up. Thus the intention is presumably to say that all men encounter or experience transcendence, but the man of biblical faith gives it a name.

As against Van Buren, then, Cox rightly suggests that our problem really is bad religion and not just bad language. (The point would be equally well taken against those who argue for the abolition of religion in favor of Christianity, capitalizing simply on a highly specialized meaning for the term "religion.") Bad religion means looking for the transcendent and seeking to experience it in the wrong way and the wrong places—for example, in supranaturalistic terms—

for God is not in that fashion to be apprehended or understood in our world at all. The problem then is how the
"transcendent" is truly to be apprehended and named. And
for this problem, Cox leaves us simply with the suggestions
that we may find a more adequate mode of symbolization in
I–You than in an I–Thou and that even the word "God" may
have to go, as we struggle on until some new name emerges.

But neither of these proposals helps us much. The latter, to
be sure, has a fine ring of humility and points to the depth of
the problem of language, but it may also be only a counsel of
despair, a call to "work, for the night is coming" without any
understanding and interpretation of the why and the for
whom of the work—and that is *theologically* irresponsible.
The idea of I–You as a substitute for I–Thou turns out, I
fear, to be a verbal gimmick. Granted that what Cox means
by an I–You relation is authentically human, granted that the
exclusive and narrow personalism surrounding the use of
I–Thou language needs to be combated, that the pietist pre-
occupation with "experiencing" God will no longer do,
granted further the principle that all our symbols for understanding the genuinely human will effect our symbolization of
God, nevertheless it remains opaque either how the I–You
formula has any special communicative value or how it helps
with the problem of naming the transcendent as Cox himself
has posed the problem.

Is there any way then to go on? I believe there is and that
in spite of a certain theological confusion and carelessness—
wrought partly by such artificial devices as the triads of tribe,
town, and technopolis, of sociological problem, political issue
and theological question, and of I–Thou, I–It, and I–You—
Cox not only is sensitive to the basic questions but touches on
fruitful lines of procedure.

A first requisite, as I have already suggested, is a more
careful distinction between the decision (or response) of
faith and the task of theological analysis and interpretation.
Whether one understands the mode of man's relation to God
to be essentially participation or confrontation or partnership
(or "alongsidedness," p. 263), whether "faith" be viewed
primarily as adoration or trust or obedience, the work of

theology as a reflective and critical discipline cannot simply
be identified with that relation, however much it may spring
from it and seek to clarify it. Theology is not identical with
doxology or recital. That is, in so far as theology has to speak
of that to which man responds, it really must and should
speak "about" God. The theologian might intend and even
formulate his work as an act of praise of God, but as theological articulation it is not simply talk "to" God. Precisely by
trying to talk intelligibly about God, theology does its work
of clarifying and assisting our response (and even talk) "to"
Him and our speaking "of" Him in witness to others (the
tasks of interpretation to ourselves and to others are not to be
separated, nor are the rules different). The "naming" of God,
in other words, cannot be an excuse for failure to engage in
the attempt to understand and interpret what is being named;
only when it is also the latter can naming serve to communicate.

But if that be so, we shall have to take up once again some
of the questions that Cox relegates to the pretechnopolitan
stage of culture, even that despised "metaphysical" kind of
theologizing. I am not thinking here of commitment to any
particular ontological or metaphysical scheme but of an order
of questioning (Cox, after all, suggests that even the anti-
metaphysics of existentialism belongs to the metaphysical
perspective). It is one thing to say that the Gospel message
cannot be tied to a particular metaphysical scheme, but quite
another to delude ourselves into supposing that we can appropriate and interpret the Gospel without any sort of "metaphysical" presuppositions or categories. Here Cox has been
quite misled by those (*e.g.*, Van Peursen) who would equate
"metaphysical thinking" with particular schemes in which
"God" is made a plug for the gaps in our knowledge or the
highest being among beings (I leave aside the question of the
historical competence of those who would identify Aquinas,
for example, with the latter view).

Indeed, if we are to take seriously Cox's protestations
about everything depending upon the question of whether
man is alone in the universe, whether God exists or not, he is
himself thoroughly committed to this further sort of interpre-

tation. The notions of "transcendence" and of "action of God" are crucial to Cox's distinguishing of his view from that of a simple nontheism—and he sees rightly in this, for without such affirmations it is difficult to see how any claim of continuity with a biblical view can be meaningful. But intelligible talk about transcendence and God's action is obviously going to involve us in a level of discussion beyond that of the pragmatic and of coordinated attack on concrete political issues. This will, again, demand talk "about" that to which man is called and invited to respond, about what is named as beyond man's possession or control and as inviting man to cooperate in common activity. However helpful the symbol I–You might prove to be in indicating a form of relation to God, for example, the "You" is not simply identical with fellow man, and it is the theological task (indispensable to communication) to explicate the convergence and the distinction. This means talk "about," even "objectifying" talk about, that which is not "an" object, which is *ex hypothesi* beyond being fully grasped by any concepts or categories ("biblical" or "metaphysical"). It means talk about existence or being, about agency and activity, and so on.

Furthermore, and wholly in accord with the central intention of *The Secular City* to deal with the world that really is, the required theological exploration cannot be a closed enterprise segregated from the rest of the modern world's explorations—especially not under the guise of being faithful to the "biblical view." If the once clear distinction of nature and supernature as neatly distinguishable levels of reality will no longer serve the purposes of theology, neither will the attempt to make a clean and unbridgeable separation between the religious statement and the nonreligious judgment.

Of course it is true that the declaration of faith (and the theological judgment) is not just the same as the historical affirmation or the moral imperative or the scientific description. But to say that questions of religious truth, and specifically questions of God, have *nothing* to do with other ways of looking at things is to be both confused and faint-hearted. This would be only another way of separating faith from the rest of life, of pressing the object of faith to the periphery or to some special place unrelated to the other places of life, and thus of encouraging the notion of its dispensability.

Christian truth can be no merely private truth. It must always seek to be publicly interpretable—and not just to an "other" public or world but to ourselves as part of that public. To try to be purely private in our theological formulations would be to have neither friends nor foes, and a Christian faith or theology that seeks to define itself out of all possible rivalry will also lose all possible support and quickly turn out to be of no possible interest.

If we are clear about these matters, then we are in a better position to distinguish the false from the genuine issues, and we can explicitly point the direction to the theological view that will support what is creative and exciting in Cox's proposals. The heart of the problem of speaking of God in the secular city, of dealing with the apparent "absence" of God, is not the supposed contrast between nonmetaphysical and metaphysical theologies. But it certainly is the problem of some very bad theologies—specifically that popular finitization of God (especially prominent in the modern, bleached Anglo-Saxon theism) and that crude supernaturalism that does indeed make God only "an" object, a being among other beings, only one agent among other agents, one present only in some experiences and not in others. It was precisely this sort of God below God, this "friend upstairs," who could be made a stop for the gaps in scientific knowledge, an explanatory principle among other principles, and who could and should have been pushed further and further to the edges of life until He became wholly technologically unemployed and unemployable.

Here is a genuinely "sociological" problem of speaking of God, a problem for which the Christian community has mostly itself to blame. But the remedy is not to be found in a retreat to inexplicable "naming" or to mere reiteration of "biblical" language or "views." It is to be found, I suggest, by taking with absolute seriousness the proposal that God is to be recognized at the center and not only at the periphery of life, by ceasing to look for God primarily in the unexplained or in the crises, and by being free to find Him everywhere in the everyday and the constant, in man's strength as well as in his weakness. But this is to say—and to require the theologian to interpret—that the action of God is to be found in every action. If God is to be met (as Thou, or You, or perhaps even as It) at the center, this can surely mean nothing less than in the totality, at every point in life and not just at some points, thus in every experience—not just in religious experience (or in "history" or even worse in *Heilsgeschichte*) but in the esthetic, the moral, and the scientific, in the impersonal as well as the personal. From such a standpoint, then, one will have to begin to explicate "transcendence" and "hiddenness and disclosure" and "action of God." And the theological questions will at this level not be "whether" but "how," and every tracing out of the how of things will be part of the depiction of God's action.

But to say this sort of thing is to take a stand not with the pale and refined theism that sees in God only the kindly and the inoffensive, or with some explicit notion of a really finite God but precisely with the magisterial theism of the Reformers, of Calvin and of Luther in the *Bondage of the Will,* and of Aquinas and Augustine, with its sense of the totality of life received in and from the hands of the Almighty. There God is not one who can be edged out from the niches He occupies. He is rather the presenter of *every* possibility, the one present (in both hiddenness and disclosure) in and through all experience and life and cosmos. Thus we may really begin with the power and presence that everywhere is, with God as the Creator of *all* things, the Orderer of all events.

Then we can come back, and with what appears to me the natural basis for Cox's statement of the matter, to the deepest level of what he calls political theology. Here is a genuine theological and ethical task, described as "that reflection-in-action by which the church finds out what this politician-God is up to and moves in to work along with Him" (p. 255). That is, by reflection on the present in the light of the events of the past which it recalls, centrally the event of Jesus Christ, and by analogy from those illuminating events, the Christian community seeks to discover the direction of God's acting. As an essential ingredient of the judgment that God is at work in all events, the question is to be asked, what is He bringing about? Here theological activity seeks to make concrete the affirmation of God's action by seeing it not as a problem of whether, but as a question of what God is up to in the technological and urban and "secular" world. About that question Cox is able to write with great eloquence and discernment, and to propose fresh and liberating directions of Christian response. But this "political issue," which is indeed a theological matter, cannot be a substitute for or be dealt with prior to or apart from the "theological question" but only in constant conjunction with it. Freed from the misguided polemic against the metaphysical (or pre- or post-metaphysical), Cox's political theology (both in the concluding chapter and throughout the book) seems to me to demand exactly a theological articulation of divine sovereignty and presence of the sort I have suggested above. In any case, I am sure that only in this direction will we find again a valid and useful way of speaking of God.

# CHAPTER 4

# How to Speak of God in a Secular Style

## Harmon R. Holcomb

*The Secular City,* as Harvey Cox gently reminds one batch of assorted critics, "was designed as a study book, intended mainly to provoke college students to discussion and not to goad bishops and seminary professors into rebuttal" (see p. 85). This modest statement of intent has been fulfilled with justified success, but it underestimates the actual accomplishments of the book as badly as it does the voracity of professors, whose appetites are, as Kierkegaard noted, longer than a tapeworm. Twanging all theological nerves still capable of a quiver, *The Secular City* is an exciting book which tempts discussion beyond its avowed limits. Having made this a compliment, I shall indulge the temptation.

To celebrate secularity in ways that are in every case on the side of the angels is no mean feat, and I alternate between admiring it and wondering how it was done. Take any subset of themes in *The Secular City* and you can follow them to your enlightenment and adopt them to your profit. Reach for the book as a whole, the interweaving of its themes, and you will embrace a fog. It is a lucidly elusive, helpfully unintelligible book.

These silly, paradoxical labels reflect my bafflement with Cox's handling of his structural thesis, namely, the relation between his theological affirmations and his social-historical interpretation of secularization. What is affirmed is elsewhere denied; what is taken away is graciously returned. One does not have to have a German passion for tidiness to be puzzled by the result. On second reflection, however, I find no contradictions, but rather a method of artificial insemination which leaves secular culture pregnant with religious meaning.

To get the structural problem before us, I shall organize a few of the themes of *The Secular City* under headings: I, the theological base; II, the description of secularity; and III, the problem of the relation between I and II. I shall then argue, IV and V, that "secularity" and its children have been baptized with religious meanings contrary to the word and spirit of the officiating minister.

## I

The theological frame of the book is sturdy, moderately orthodox, with family ties to Barth, Gollwitzer, and Gogarten. Sovereign God is free to be Himself and is not to be identified with man or any human quality or any historical situation. He meets men as the wholly Other, the author of their identity, the center and source of value, working to liberate men to enjoy the creation. Always hidden and always present, God elects men to be His sons and partners and gives the fullest possible disclosure of this partnership in Jesus. Undetectable by empirical methods and undiscoverable by clear thinking, God is known through a personal decision of faith and is named "God" by grasping, via the biblical witness, the same reality whom the Hebrews called Yahweh and whom the Disciples saw in Jesus. Today the secular city supplies the new occasion in which the Gospel calls us to discern the signs of the Kingdom and to respond to our neighbor appropriately (pp. 112, 121, 199, 243, 259–262, 264).

## II

In contrast, the description of secularity is what gives the book its impact and immediacy. Secularization is "the loosing of the world from religious and quasi-religious understandings of itself. . . . the breaking of all supernatural myths and sacred symbols." History is defatalized, metaphysics is discarded, all forms of otherworldliness die without notice or care, and men no longer look to religious rules or morality for meaning.

The authentic consequence of biblical faith, an irreversible secularization grows in the urban context to form a pluralistic society in which men are incurably pragmatic and countenance only pragmatic truths. They do not ask "ultimate questions" about "boundary situations," for instance, about *the* meaning of their lives or of history. Man is the source of meaning and value, the creator of his cosmos, and he feels no anxiety over the death of the God of theism, whether classical or Tillichian. The "religious" stage of history has ended; man is becoming man, and the world is becoming "mere world." We have come of age (*cf.* pp. 2–5, 17, 20–21, 69, 72–81, 207, 253).

### III

That a problem exists in relating the theological base to the description of secularity is clear when one sets the statements made in I alongside those made in II. Both, it seems, just cannot be true. Given the glad, emphatic proclamation of secularity along with the less emphatic, scattered use of the theological frame, many readers have read *The Secular City* with the weight of interpretation falling on secularity. This yields a plausible misinterpretation, once my own.

### a.

When we give the description of secularity the governing role, we get a tasty, secular birthday cake with theological icing which does not add much. For example, posit pragmatic man, believing in nothing final, confident in his world where he creates the values, distrustful of overarching schemes, and uninterested in "ultimate questions"—well, why should he be any more interested in Cox's chattering about God and the Covenant and Easter than in any other quaint adventure in God-talk? If we can translate the Bible into the language of history, sociology, and politics, then the Bible is eminently dispensable. If "God" is ambiguous and irrelevant to the point of meaninglessness (p. 241), then no act of faith will endow a meaningless term with meaning.

While plausible, the foregoing interpretation rests on the initial error of giving the characteristics of secularization a weight which Cox never intended. He has no desire to reduce the Bible to sociological truths about the city or to tailor the Gospel to fit the shape of modern man. That Cox omits some biblical motifs is true, as Charles West has sensitively indicated with reference to the Cross, sin, alienation, and death (see pp. 59–63). But, as Cox's appreciative response to West suggests, a modification of the book can take account of these admittedly serious omissions.

b.

What, then, is Cox's method of resolving the prima-facie incompatibility between the theological base and secularity? Cox himself is less than clear about this, and when he comes in Part Four (pp. 241–269) to speak directly to one form of the question, his answer seems strained and off the point, like a theological addendum to a book about something else. Thus he begins with a syllogism which, in a case still pending, dies of either therapeutic or illegal abortion:

(1) "If man cannot speak of God in the secular city, then all we have said about secularization as the work of God for man is nonsense and the whole thesis of the book is erroneous."

(2) ". . . the word 'God' means almost nothing to modern secular man. His mental world and his way of using language is such that he can neither understand nor use the word 'God' meaningfully" (p. 241).

This looks like a syllogism of the form: if *p*, then *q; p*, therefore . . . , and we wait for the *q* (*i.e.*, "then all we have said . . . is nonsense," etc.), but the conclusion never comes. It does not and should not come, because Cox in practice weakens the second premise almost beyond recognition. This is tantamount to saying that he transforms the whole description of secularization on which premise (2) rests, with the unnerving consequence that all of his descriptions of secular man must be taken at considerably less than their face value. Secularity has connotations undreamed of in our sociologies. Either this, the inflation of secularity, or the plausible misinterpretation discussed earlier is the correct one after all.

Before developing this, let us look at how Cox handles the problem in the pages following the syllogism. He takes a druidic saying of Bonhoeffer's to the effect that we do not speak about God at all, but "name" Him. The theory of naming invoked in support is notable mainly for ignoring the difficulties which have made theologians as diverse as Thomas, Kierkegaard, and Hartshorne reluctant to regard "God" as a proper name. In addition, the theory never faces the usual difficulties in relating names to descriptive phrases.

The first consequence of this account of naming (which is not identical with the fine exegetical account used earlier on pp. 73–76) is that naming is a "sociological" problem. The truistic grounds for holding this are that human beings can not speak unless they have memories, histories, and meanings. *All* linguistic events become, by this tactic, innocuously sociological, and both sociology and naming are gutted of content. The original problem posed by the two premises remains untouched, if indeed the commentary (pp. 243–248) does not strengthen the second premise and cause further wonder as to why the conclusion (the thesis of the book is erroneous) is not drawn.

A more important way of naming God is "politically," by "participating in that political action by which He restores men to each other in mutual concern and responsibility. . . . Standing in a picket line is a way of speaking" (p. 256). This form of speaking, done in the light of God's acts in the Exodus and at Easter, truly exemplifies a biblical lesson about knowing and serving God. As an answer to the problem of Cox's two premises, it is irrelevant, since his own second premise forbids reference to God, the Exodus, and Easter. God is served in all acts of love and justice, but He is "named" only if language can meaningfully refer an act to Him.

If political naming were the heart of Cox's answer, a fatal reductionism would be unintentionally present. We can observe a just act and join in it, but unless there is a language capable of connecting the act with the intent to delight God, we can infer nothing more than that we are comrades with a man of goodwill. Simply qua act, no act names God or witnesses to anything beyond the character of the human agent, and even his motives and self-understanding cannot be inferred with any certainty. A publicly used and taught language in which "God" occurs essentially and meaningfully is a necessary condition of there being political naming of God in the secular style. Premise (2) denies the possibility of just such a language.

All of us feel the force of the second premise, the descriptive truth in it, and Cox is concerned with the ambiguity and irrelevance of most of our Christian language and forms of worship rather than with upholding a technical, positivistic thesis about meaninglessness. I agree with his concern and the direction of it, but it is, nevertheless, misleading to describe secular man as he does and then invite that man to understand himself and his deity in the light of God's acts at Exodus and Easter. So I return to the theme that, while Cox may use secularity like a club in his polemical sections, he uses it like a balloon when a little soaring is required.

IV

The theological frame of the book is, as Cox makes clear, prior and necessary and determinative. This results in a reinterpretation of secularity, a fact which Cox leaves obscured.

Methodologically, *The Secular City* is an essay in "theological reflection," scrutinizing the events confronting us in the light of the Bible and endeavoring to use the secular city as a symbol which is shaped and judged by its faithfulness to the doctrine of the Kingdom of God (pp. 110, 254). Descriptively, the whole account in the early chapters of the new form of society is, Cox says, an interpretation which rests on biblical categories (pp. 54, 108–109). Ethically, the city is the occasion for the summons of the Gospel to a new common life, but the city is not the source of the summons. It is God who liberates us from cultural deities like The Girl and from values which "have no ultimacy." Responsibility and freedom are *given* to secular man by the One who is the source of freedom and value (pp. 121, 197–199, 202–204, 215).

Ontologically, God supplies "that framework of limitation within which alone freedom has any meaning." Without Him, man cannot be man, for the elements of our humanity and very identity are His gifts. He holds the world together so that it may be explored with confidence (pp. 66, 199, 259, 261).

Religiously (for want of a better term), secular man experiences this transcendent God at those hard edges of experience which are not at our disposal. We can say yes or no to the ("ultimate"?) questions of whether we are alone in the universe, whether our responsibility is given to us or self-created, and whether in Jesus Christ "we know who God is and what human life is for" (pp. 204, 243, 260–262). These are what we used to call, before *The Secular City*, religious decisions based on religious experience and spoken of via a religious use of language which marks the difference between God and all else.

V

If the theological base is prior, necessary, and determinative of the meaning of secularity on the levels of methodology, description, ethics, ontology, and religion, then the structural problem is solved. It dissolves and evaporates by definition, for secularity includes all those things whose imagined absence generated the problem. Everything is given back.

Secular man *can* experience the transcendent and order his cosmos around it, thus reintroducing the essentials of the sacred-profane dichotomy. Modern man *does* ask those questions formerly called ultimate questions about boundary situations, forcing us to conclude that he is *homo religiosus*, erroneously listed as dead. There *is* a *telos* of history, a general purpose running through the plurality of historical patterns to which secular historiography is restricted, but which secular man can transcend in faith.

The quintessence of what is irrelevant to pragmatic man, namely the One who is never at our disposal and can never be manipulated, can be known by pragmatic man to be the *prius* of there being pragmatic truths at all. This is a rich pragmatism indeed, making one wonder if it is not merely a form of modern piety to hold that an unexamined metaphysic is the only one worth living. In any case, with a pragmatism of this sort it is not surprising that pragmatic ethics turn out to depend on theological ethics.

It is also the case that secular man *needs* God. True, the God he needs is no "working hypothesis," but then He never was, in spite of the foolish, historically inaccurate phrase foisted upon popular discussion by Bonhoeffer in a careless moment. Cox's splendid criticism of sacred language used in religious ghettos to meet private religious needs is a cheering destruction of the idols. Just as surely, *The Secular City* shows by indirection that there are valid senses in which men may be said to need God.

I conclude that it is not difficult to be both moderately orthodox and robustly secular if you pack into your one world everything for which traditional theology supposedly needed two. In this dialogue between faith and culture, the voice of an unbelieving culture is muffled and ends by squeaking a tune called by faith. The dialogue which we need is, I think, different and more difficult. The Bible says that God gives everything back to the man of faith, but we should not presume to do it for God. When an author emulates the miracle of the loaves and fishes, easily and quickly providing enough for everyone, the result is not miracle but magic. And, as all secular men know, magic is mainly legerdemain.

Rather than dwelling upon the praiseworthy achievements of *The Secular City*, I have argued that it is an instructive failure at the very point at which so admirable a theologian as Paul Lehmann finds it most helpful. The failure comes in the attempt to perform a direct marriage between biblical categories and the deliverances of social-historical studies, and I find the consequent confusion instructive because its presence reinforces four convictions of my own. We cannot avoid the *general* problem of how language can refer to God by playing favorites among the species but damning "religious language" and exempting historial and social vocabularies from the problem. We cannot endow social-historical analyses with hidden biblical meanings. We cannot make a direct translation from historical-political categories into biblical categories, and vice versa. We *do* require a generalized bridge-language of the kind once supplied by metaphysics and ontology.

To say this is to confess that the case is difficult, even desperate, since traditional metaphysical systems are today a liability, and modern ventures are regarded as at least as dubious as the biblical language which they are supposed to illumine. Still, this is the alternative which might preserve Cox's host of valid insights. In fact, an implicit ontology already seems to inform his book and to peer out here and there between the very lines that proclaim the death of metaphysics and its ilk.

# PART FIVE

# HARVEY COX RESPONDS

# Afterword

*Harvey Cox*

One of my reasons for writing *The Secular City* was to challenge a popular misconception about the relation of theological reflection to practical life. I had noticed that many serious people in the heady and demanding world of day-to-day decision making in our urban civilization suspect that theology is something for the cloister or for the groves of academe. They think of it as a highly esoteric specialty with no relevance whatever to the issues they face. Oddly enough, I found that many theologians shared this prejudice. Jealous of their prerogatives as specialists and often insecure among both the *hommes d'affaires* and the poor people, they had convinced themselves that theology probably had, in fact, little interest to anyone but theologians.

I strongly differ with this view of the place and purpose of theology. I recognize that theological work demands a degree of training and skill equivalent to that of any other discipline. But I also believe that the *reason* for theology's existence is the critical nurture of the whole historical community whose symbols and practices theologians investigate. My own theological perspective leads me to discount any supernatural "overhead" or "God-out-there." Thus, for me, the theological enterprise seeks to grasp the problems man faces in this historic present in the light of his past and his future, that is in light of faith and hope. Without the stimulus and prodding of theology, in this sense of the word, life becomes unreflective, ahistorical and provincial. It can degenerate into a kind of moral and spiritual astigmatism, or more accurately, a near-sightedness in which nothing is seen in any real perspective.

But without a continual conversation with the real world, theology itself also suffers. It becomes effete, trivial and precious. Thus *The Secular City* was written in an attempt to get theologians to open their eyes to the secular world and to get those who inhabit this secular world to understand it and themselves in a historical-theological perspective.

I had wanted to write such a book for some time. The actual occasion for putting it on paper came when the National Student Christian Federation asked me to prepare a study book for its conferences in 1965. I accepted their invitation and went to work, but quickly found that the format imposed some real limitations. Several times during the writing, my editor had to reprimand me about the vocabulary and the level of the argument, reminding me that I should aim for the average college sophomore. Many times, in the interest of lucidity and clarity, I regretfully chopped out the kind of qualifications and balancing judgments which contribute to both the accuracy and the dullness of most theological writing.

Still, I think writing the book in this way turned out to have been best after all. The publisher printed 10,000 copies, a considerable number for religious books, and put it in a paperback edition.

I still do not understand the somewhat incredible attention the book has received. At this writing there are a quarter million copies in print of the American paperback edition alone. There is a British edition (published by SCM Press), and there will soon be Finnish, German, Dutch, Korean, French and Swedish editions. In a few months the revised version of the American edition will appear—this time in a hard cover. Obviously students are not the only people concerned about these ideas.

The best thing about having one's book widely read is that a large volume of criticisms, reviews and responses stimulate the writer to rethink his thesis. The present collection of essays and reviews has contributed immeasurably to the revising and rethinking process. These criticisms have helped me correct and reformulate my own argument. I am sure they have also sparked clearer reflection and uncovered new men-

tal vistas for their readers. Since the kind of theological thinking we will need in the coming secular epoch will demand the
disciplined imagination of numberless minds I am delighted
to see so many gifted people wrestling with the same issues
which challenge and bewilder me.

It is regrettable, however, that the logistics of a book such
as this prevent me from doing justice to all the articles it
contains. Needless to say, I have been unsettled and stimu-
lated by all of them, but absorbing and responding to them
individually would be the work of the next ten years of my
life and would far exceed the space allotted to me here.

In revisiting *The Secular City* I shall restrict myself first to
listing some points at which I have already been forced both
by the logic of my critics and by my own experiences in the
past two years to modify my position considerably. I
shall then register those convictions about which I feel even
more strongly now than I did then, sometimes despite the
efforts of many resourceful and vigorous critics to lead me to
repentence. I shall close with a wistful resumé of how I hope
some of my presently unsolved problems might be overcome.

Here, then, are changes I would make were I writing *The
Secular City* over again today.

1) Several critics ask whether myth and metaphysics are
really gone from the secular city, or should be. I still hold
that myth and metaphysics spring from the tribal and town
stages of societal development, but I now believe that they
also have some real value for secular man. Here those critics
who remind me of the human significance of ritual and cultus
even in a secular age have been highly persuasive. Rabbi
Rubenstein is the most persuasive of all. He is right to inform
me that it is not a mark of the truly mature man or of the
authentically mature society to jettison its past with the kind
of ruthlessness found here and there in *The Secular City*.

The fact is that I never really intended to argue for a
flippant disposal of the past. Some of my critics see this and
take me to task for seeing continuities where none exist (*i.e.*,
Max Stackhouse and George Peck). I did want the book to
express a critical continuity with the Judeo-Christian tradi-

tion and its recurrent theological motifs. Ruel Tyson sees more clearly than most readers that *The Secular City's* "recurrent theme is that of return to origins," a *"regressus ad originem."* Tyson also mentions my colleague psychologist-sociologist Erik Erikson. Erikson's work is crucial in the problem of relating past to present. He has written brilliantly about the various identity crises in the life of an individual, occurring at the oedipal, adolescent, young adult and other nodal points in the life cycle. Erikson believes that the key to a successful negotiation of an identity crisis is the individual's creative reappropriation of his previous identities into a new one which stands in continuity with the past but is now freed to deal with the future. Either to be bound to one's past or to reject it all out of hand is wrong. Both are symptoms of an unstable identity.

I think the same reasoning can apply to societies as well as to individuals. That culture which ruthlessly rejects the memories of its tribe and town past entirely, which tries to live in the technopolitan age *de nouveau,* is doomed to superficiality and directionlessness. Only as it accepts and reorganizes its mythical and metaphysical past into a cultural identity open to an unpredictable future will a society be prepared to cope with that future.

This does not mean, of course, that myth and metaphysics can play in the secular city the kind of unitive and integrative functions they once played. When myth is recognized to be myth it is already consigned to a lower status. Once metaphysics is understood as one among many historically conditioned ways of symbolizing reality, it loses the absolute claims once made for it. Neither myth nor metaphysics can play the commanding role they played in the epochs in which they emerged. But just because they cannot perform their original function is no reason why they cannot perform other humane and important functions.

Modern dance provides a good example. Dance is a thrilling repristination in our time of the mimetic-expressive style of coping with the human environment characteristic of the tribal moment in man's pilgrimage. Dance exudes a lusty primitive sensuousness and erotic exhilaration which im-

measurably enrich the life of urban man. Dance was originally a rhythmic myth told by the body, a somatic symbol.
Today the myth is broken, but the movement remains a powerful way of strengthening our oneness with our own bodies,
a relationship often eroded by our technological life style;
and this happens both to dancers and to audiences since both
are in some way involved in the mimetic reality. Mimesis also
strengthens the powers of imagination, so it is possible that a
rebirth of mimesis in our time may help us bridge the dangerous imagination gap which cuts us off from people, like
the Chinese, who are in many ways so different from us. It
may help us develop the capacity to feel and see things from
the other person's point of view. This dance and mime may
help us do. But they cannot integrate the whole culture as
they could for tribal peoples. Mime is one among other
human activities, not the focus of everything. Still it *is* tribal
in origin and it *does* belong in the secular city. Without its
tribal past continuing to live in its present, life in the secular
city would be duller and far less colorful. But his tribal past
is not present for secular man as something which organizes
his universe for him. It is present as one among many sources
of emotional enlargement and personal enrichment. When he
"returns" to it through the dance, music or art of the tribe
(and the cinematic experience, as Marshall McLuhan has
pointed out, has important tribal features), he returns only in
imagination and only temporarily so that his life in the secular city is a zestier one. When a person tries to return permanently to a tribal personality, or a society tries to organize
itself as a tribe (as Nazi Germany did), then we know a
pathological relapse has taken place.

My own work in the future will be devoted in large measure to reexamining the characteristically "religious" practices
of man in an effort to see what elements can be used in the
interests of humanization and social change. I hope this will
deliver me to some extent from the "puritan" bias Rabbi
Richard Rubenstein detects and rightly calls into question.

Incidentally, speaking of Richard Rubenstein, it puzzles me
that he can offer such a brilliant and telling criticism from a
Jewish perspective without a trace of invective, while Steven

Schwarzschild found it necessary to compose such a polemical tirade that I am sure he himself will be embarrassed when he reads it in a quieter moment. The purple hue of Schwarzschild's words and the obvious disproportion between the intensity of emotion he displays and the question at issue suggest that he is not really attacking me but is using this occasion to vent his feelings about many things, feelings that have been accumulating for a long time. I will content myself, therefore, with pointing out that I have seldom encountered such a grotesque misreading of *The Secular City*. By lumping me with some vague thing he labels "the new immanentism," Schwarzschild makes me say that "the world is God; therefore let the world become as it will." Even the most casual reader of *The Secular City* knows that this is the exact opposite of my thesis. What I said was that since the world is *not* God (desacralization, deconsecration), it is our responsibility to shape and steer it. Schwarzschild shows this low regard for accuracy throughout his philippic. He is so angry that what I actually say about something has only casual interest. For example, if he had read my sharp criticism of those business organizations which try to make themselves over into pseudofamilies he would know that I share his disgust with the "familial" rhetoric and "big-brother" policies he rightly assails in General Electric and McDonnell Aircraft. But he seems to believe that by slugging them he is bashing me too. The only safe thing to do when someone is acting this way is to step aside until he has triumphed over all the things he is against and then hope that a conversation can begin.

If a conversation could begin, I would agree with Schwarzschild that Christian theologians have been wrong in confusing the YHWH of the Bible with a *deus* or *theos*. In fact this is what I thought I said in *The Secular City*. If he could stop shouting, we might quietly discuss the translation of Exodus 3:14. Though my interpretation of the text may not be to Schwarzschild's liking, it is in no sense "an entirely new version." The Hebrew verb in question can mean "to be," or "cause to be, perform, do." I got the idea he refers to from Bernhard Anderson's *Understanding the Old Testament* (Englewood Cliffs: Prentice-Hall, Inc., 1959, p. 34). I would

refer interested readers to W. F. Albright's discussion in
*From Stone Age to Christianity* (Garden City: Doubleday &
Company, Inc., 1957, pp. 196–199). If he could sit still,
Schwarzschild and I might talk together about whether the
whole Old Testament can really be called monotheistic. It is
hard to read about Elijah's contest with the prophets of Baal
without seeing some evidence that the existence of other
deities is not denied. Perhaps the very idea of monotheism
represents a projection of later philosophical categories into a
Bible interested in something different, a practice we moderns
have indulged in too often.

Still, I am afraid that even in the calmest atmosphere,
Schwarzschild and I would finally disagree, for he goes on to
say: "Why then does Cox propound such nonsense? Because
he has to justify the thesis that the God of the Bible is the
God of Christianity . . ." If Schwarzschild rightly locates
the real nub of my error then I must plead guilty. I *do* believe
that the God of the Hebrew Bible, the God of Abraham,
Isaac and Jacob is indeed the God and Father of Jesus of
Nazareth. But here my perversity is not mine alone. It has
been shared by almost all Christians (except the Montanists)
and by many Jews for two thousand years.

I look forward intensely to the coming dialogue between
Christians and Jews. I rejoice that very few Jews will exact
as a precondition of the conversation my accepting Schwarzschild's definition of my reprobacy. To do so would be to
surrender the whole faith before the dialogue begins, which
no conversation partner can justifiably expect.

To return to the point, myth has a place in the life of
secular man. So does metaphysics. With the emergence
of historicism, with our conscious awareness of the
sociocultural conditioning under which all philosophical
speculation occurs, the classical enterprise of metaphysics,
as carried on by Aristotle and Saint Thomas is surely over.
These men wove intellectual systems with sufficient symbolic
power and complexity to integrate whole cultural periods.
Metaphysicians cannot be expected to perform that function
in the twentieth century. Today we integrate our specialities
operationally by joining other specialists in focusing them on

issues we will have to solve in order to continue to exist. Though we must still explore the implications of our ways of thinking—and do so with all the vigor we can summon—it is hard to imagine how our findings could ever produce the cultural edifice these men did.

But metaphysics itself need not die. Though the function he once played has been preempted, the metaphysician need not be cast on the ash heap. Metaphysical questions can and should still be raised. The smugness of cultural assumptions should be challenged. The tendency of a pragmatic society to absolutize its pragmatism should be exposed and needled. Indeed, metaphysics in the secular city will probably play a role nearly opposite that which it played in preceding eras. In our time the metaphysicians, instead of integrating our lives for us, will probably more often challenge the premature integrations and cultural foreclosures that constrict us. They will play more a critical than a constructive role, to ask *why* and *what for* when such questions upset the technological mentality. For this reason, metaphysics in the secular city will probably be done more frequently by the poet and the movie maker, by the novelist and the playwright, than by the academic philosopher or theologian.

Metaphysics, like myth, is part of the past of our race and therefore is a part of each of us. If we insist on allowing it to organize our complex symbolic universe for us or if we junk it completely we shall be the poorer for it. The adult who has never grown up or the one who never allows himself to be stretched by the experiences and hopes of his past both are impoverished. Our task today is to transmute the answers of classical metaphysics into questions that will guard the openness of our symbol worlds today.

2) A second point at which both the probes of the critics and my own experiences have forced me to rethink my position has to do with the organizational-institutional church. Again, I never intended to be anti-institutional, anarchistic or individualistic in *The Secular City*, but at times I allowed myself to use phrases which gave people that impression. I realize that the church is not pure spirit and cannot live in the modern world, or in any world for that matter, without some

institutional expression. Nor is "institution" just a necessary evil. Institutions, as Arnold Gehlen has shown in his studies of the subject, really serve to liberate man rather than to imprison him. Institution is for man what instinct is for animal. Institutions make it possible for the organism to deal with certain levels of decisions by answering a whole range of questions before they are asked. The animal flees or freezes in the presence of danger without cogitating about it. It is a reflex action. Man goes through most of his life thinking only of day-to-day questions. He does not decide each morning whether family, property and the nation state (all arrangements unknown to animals) deserve his support and cooperation. Mostly, he goes to work, supports his family, drives his car, without much thought about the institutional assumptions that underlie these activities. In fact, if he had to think them through every time he acted, he would be like the centipede who became paralyzed when someone asked him how he moved all those legs at once. He would never get to anything else.

But we are not just centipedes. Sometimes we do question our assumptions about property or nation states. And sometimes we ask about the church as an institution. We do this because we now realize that property is not, as many once thought, an "order of creation" and that nations have no validity grounded in some natural law. Likewise, I believe that all the forms of institutional life we find in the church are open to change. There is no structure or practice so sacred that it is above critical reflection. Denominations? Residential parishes? Professional clergy? All these are institutional forms which arose in particular historical circumstances, to serve certain purposes. They can be altered or discarded if need be. But again, mere discarding will hardly suffice. What we need now is a willingness to *reinstitutionalize* the forms of church life based on a conscious theological recognition of what the church's purpose is.

In our search for forms of church life congruous with our changing urban civilization, Dr. Stackhouse's suggestion that we reexamine the model of covenantal communities is highly apposite. Covenants have just the kind of provisionality, openness and emphasis on God's disclosure of Himself "where community-forming powers are at work" we need today. In any case, structure should always serve purpose, and too many of our present structures, preeminently the denominations, have long since outlived their usefulness and have become dysfunctional.

One phrase that helps clarify the point comes from a recent World Council document that criticizes "structural fundamentalism," an attitude of rigid unwillingness to recognize the historically conditioned character of the forms of church life. "Structural fundamentalism" is analogous to the biblical fundamentalism which refuses to allow any investigation of the historical sources of texts. Biblical fundamentalists believe this would destroy the Bible. We have found however, that a historical-critical view of the Bible has deepened, not destroyed, our respect for its truth. Likewise, a readiness to recognize the historical sources and social determinants of forms of church life will free us to change and modify where the mission demands it. We will no longer need to cling obsessively to outmoded structures the way fundamentalists cling to an unchanging and magical view of a text.

Although the evidence today is still not terribly encouraging, I am impressed by the willingness of some people in the church to change and reexamine traditional patterns. This happens wherever the apparatus of the church begins to be viewed as something intended to serve the peace and justice of the world rather than to bolster the status of the church itself. The Vatican Council itself is one of the most striking examples. When I was writing *The Secular City* it was still not clear how far the council would go. Today, though it will take years to apply the council's decisions, few people would deny that the spirit of *aggiornamento* is truly regnant. There are also indications that the Pope may begin to use his far-flung diplomatic empire, originally designed to secure the interests of the Catholic Church, as a system for building world community and keeping open the channels of negotiation. The National Council of Churches has thrilled some people and angered others by periodically committing its institutional strength and prestige in matters where one might

have expected the conservatism of the churches to prevent
action. In the past two years, the National Council has supported a controversial ministry in the Mississippi Delta in the
teeth of much determined opposition. It has made a substan-
tial contribution to the passage of national civil-rights legisla-
tion. It has come out publicly in criticism of the Johnson
administration's policy in Vietnam and one of its study conferences boldly called for the recognition of Communist China
as a step toward world peace. These actions have all proved
to me that church institutions need not necessarily become
mere captives of their own sclerotic structures but can adapt
and move.

Also, at the level of presbyteries, city councils of churches
and even local congregations, there is some evidence that real
institutional change is possible. True, most church organizations at every level remain self-centered and immobile. But
here and there a council of churches like the one in Roch-
ester, New York, tools up to support the poor in their battle
for justice in the city; a local church, like the First English
Lutheran in Columbus, uses its staff and property to
strengthen the voice of the disenfranchised and persecuted.
Though it is wrong to be sanguine, one cannot relapse into
total pessimism about the church's role in the secular city
when these examples are considered.

This, then, represents my thinking to date on the place of
myth, metaphysics and the institutional church in the secular
city. I have been told that *The Secular City* is a very puritan
book. I accept that designation and would suggest that we
have needed a period of antiseptic puritanism to free us from
the tyrannical spirits and schemes of our ancestors. The
puritan always wants to cleanse, scour and eliminate—keeping only what is utterly essential. In his ardor he may toss out
things that many people would want to retain. After his
work is done others may reclaim some of the valuables from
the dust bin just the way some of us like to keep pot-bellied
stoves or eiderdown quilts. It is not that we are against oil
heat, but we like and need things in our lives which keep us in
touch with the past even when their original function has been
largely left behind. This is certainly the case with myth, and

one could probably say the same thing about "religion." A period of "neoorthodoxy," of selective reappropriation of once oppressively inhibitive images, is possible only after a long and successful period of critical "liberalism." Religion, like myth and metaphysics, is a human phenomenon and should be accepted as such, neither more nor less, by the secular man. But there is no reason why a *truly* secular man, one who is no longer haunted by dead gods, needs to continue to cauterize his consciousness. Depriving ourselves of the satisfaction and stimulation afforded by the symbolic riches of the past is a worthless form of asceticism. The city will only be truly secular when it can welcome them back into its life without fear, when it can accept them and use them as the human things they are.

## II

When I turn to those parts of *The Secular City* I would affirm even more emphatically today, the first would be the basically positive evaluation of the process of secularization. Today I feel more strongly than ever that the secularization should not be viewed as an example of massive and catastrophic cultural backsliding but as a product of the impact of the biblical faith itself on world civilization. When I first wrote *The Secular City*, this thesis, though it had been presented to European readers by, among others, the German theologian Friedrich Gogarten, still seemed shocking and even sensational to many American readers. Since then, however, similar arguments have appeared in English, some of them by people on whose untranslated work I had relied in my own research. Perhaps the best is the impressive volume by Arend van Leeuwen entitled *Christianity and World History* (New York: Charles Scribner's Sons, 1965). I had met Professor van Leeuwen and read some of his shorter papers before writing my own book, but this encyclopedic volume was published only after *The Secular City* appeared. In it van Leeuwen makes a point very comparable to mine but does it with scholarly erudition and historical documentation immeasurably beyond my own. His thesis is that one can distin-

guish between "ontocratic" and "theocratic" cultures, and
that only in the latter are secularization and social change
really possible. He believes that the biblical faith, often borne
on the vehicle of Western culture, opens the windows in
impeditive ontocratic cultures and looses them for the adventure of world history. Van Leeuwen believes that in Christianity and secularization we really see two branches of the
same tree, two interdependent forces stemming from the
same historical root.

Some have criticized van Leeuwen's typology of ontocratic
and theocratic cultures as being too rigid and restrictive.
Similar criticisms have been made of my tribe-town-
technopolis typology. I would not want to defend my typology, which was intended merely as a useful device for
organizing the material, and van Leeuwen would probably
feel the same. In fact, the only serious question I would have
about van Leeuwen's book is whether he has really proved
that secularization has uniquely Western sources or whether
there are not highly analogous currents to be found, for example, in certain periods of Japanese Buddhism. It may be
that van Leeuwen's theological starting point, for which he
relies heavily on Karl Barth and Hendrik Kraemer, has led
him to assume the utter uniqueness of biblical faith where
another equally competent scholar might find striking parallels in non-Christian religions. This is not a major weakness,
however, and van Leeuwen's book remains the best cor-
roboration of the main thesis of *The Secular City* I know
about.

But van Leeuwen's book is not the only one. Especially
impressive is the recent work of Roman Catholic scholars on
this issue. Several years ago, Alfons Auer, then professor of
Roman Catholic moral theology at the University of Würz-
burg, published a book entitled *Der Weltoffener Christ*, by
which some of the themes of my own book were inspired. On
my widely criticized thesis that Christians should *support* the
secularization process, I have had encouragement in the consistently excellent work of Professor Johannes Metz, another
Catholic, who teaches theology at the University of Münster.
Metz recently wrote: ". . . to Christianize the world means

in its basic sense to make the world more worldly, to bring it to its own . . . In its saving power, grace calls and guides [things] from their sinful estrangement into their own. It calls and guides the world into its perfect secularism." ("A Believer's Look at the World: A Christian Standpoint in the Secularized World," in *The Christian and the World* ed. by M. Ferro-Calvo *et al.*, New York: [P. J. Kenedy & Sons, 1965], p. 93.)

More recently, the influential Jesuit theologian Karl Rahner has dedicated some of his writing to the Christian sources of secularization and the obligation of Christians to view it favorably.

> If the world of the future is a world of rational planning, a demythologized world, a world secularized by the creature in order that it may serve as the raw material for man's activity, then this whole modern attitude—no matter what particular elements in it we may be able and ought to criticize—is basically a Christian one ("Christianity and the New Man," in *Ibid.*, p. 228n).

Still, the process of secularization is not an unqualified good. I wish to affirm a direction in history, even a process of evolutionary differentiation in the history of religion. But I want to avoid a simple "progress view." Here the image of the crap game, which I originally borrowed from Archie Hargreaves and which drew numberless comments, both positive and negative, will help. I would argue that secularization "raises the stakes" of the game. It puts man in a position where he can do more harm and more good, where his mistakes will be costlier and his virtues will be more salutary than ever before. Secularization means increased control by man over his physical environment, deepened knowledge of his own inner workings, mightier weapons, more powerful medicines, higher aspirations, the need for more accountability. The secularization of the world is a summons to man to grow up. He can still refuse. But his refusal in our time would be incomparably more catastrophic than in any previous period.

Another point at which I would not only decline to retreat but might even wish to sharpen the question has to do with those criticisms of my willingness to identify certain movements and events in our time with the breaking in of the Kingdom of God. I would want to reiterate my insistence that in the secular city itself we can discern certain provisional elements of the promised Kingdom. Some reviewers have sniffed occasionally about my "sectarian" bias, or my propensity to overlook the bad things that are there in the city, like the loneliness which accompanies anonymity or the alienation which results from too much mobility.

I am not averse to being classed as a sectarian. I know full well that there are things about the secular city that are wrong and unjust. But I am displeased about the fact that the theological conversation has been dominated for some time now by the theological insights of the "magisterial reformation," the "mainline" protestant traditions of Luther, Calvin and the Anglicans. This has been true even though American church life traces its roots more to the left-wing reformers than to the mainline. I believe that the sectarian contribution must now be restated and must become a partner in the dialogue. I would agree that the radical tradition in Protestant theology must be tempered by a Lutheran respect for the provisional autonomy of the secular, a Calvinist interest in the constancy to God's action for man and perhaps an Anglican respect for the continuities which link past to present. But these traditions need, in turn, to be challenged by the sectarian. Some sectarians withdrew from the political realm, some became quietists, but the sectarians who interest me were those who wanted the reformation to change the society, not just the church. The magisterial reformers never really followed the logical consequences of their reformation into its radical implications for the social order. This was left for the Anabaptists, Congregationalists, Quakers and others to press. The mainline reformers never developed a viable theology for social change, one of the most nagging needs of the modern church. Perhaps a reaffirmation of this half-suppressed tradition will help us with this problem today.

True, sectarians have sometimes made the mistake of identifying marks of the Kingdom too quickly. They have often been wrong in their confession. But we have just come through a period of theological ethics in which our error lay in quite the opposite direction. Chastised rightly by Reinhold Niebuhr for putting too much hope in mere political solutions, for being too sentimentally impressed by idealistic schemes, we learned to put great emphasis on the complexity and difficulty of all moral issues. We saw the Kingdom of God as an "impossible possibility," as a transcendent standard of judgment by which the pretensions of our petty human plans could be exposed.

But perhaps we learned our lesson too well. In trying to avoid moral oversimplification we saw more ambiguity than anyone else. In guarding the Kingdom of God from ideological perversion, we rendered it politically irrelevant. To say that the Kingdom of God is not of this earth is true—but only half true. It is also "in the midst of us." It is among us like mustard seed and yeast. Its first fruits can be tasted even now. It not only empowers us to say no to the pride and pretense of man; it also allows us to say yes where the Messianic era breaks in on the darkened world. It requires us to be specific not only in our condemnations but in what we support. Though this can produce mistakes and will require constant repentance and reexamination, nothing is so morally wrong as phrasing one's moral concerns in general terms when the situation requires the specific.

I appreciate more than I can say the attention which thoughtful critics have lavished on *The Secular City*. Their comments, even when most negative, flattered and pleased me. They often helped me to strengthen my argument here and there. But as for the basic thesis of the book, that secularization should be welcomed as an occasion requiring maturity in man, here I still stand; I can take no other.

## III

Finally, I come to the issue which has fascinated me most since the publication of *The Secular City*. It is the one dealt with in the final chapter, entitled "To Speak in a Secular

Fashion of God." I concede that this chapter does not fully accomplish its purpose. My only defense is that the failure is not wholly mine but is shared by the entire theological community. For years the doctrine of God in theology has become more and more problematical. We have ignored or passed over it, but our sloth has now returned to haunt us. It serves us right, I think, that our shirking the work we should have done on the problem of God has now produced the widely celebrated "death-of-God" movement in theology which, if it makes no constructive contribution toward extricating us from the quagmire, dramatizes with chilling cogency the bankruptcy of the categories we have been trying to use.

The "death of God" means different things to different theologians. For some it means the final disappearance of that divinity which had been perched at the fulcrum of our classical metaphysical systems. Insofar as we have confused this abstract deity with watered-down versions of the biblical Yahweh, often welding the two together, it signals his demise too. For others, the "death of God" denotes the disappearance of those familiar and culturally prescribed ways of encountering the numinous which touched our forefathers but no longer reach us. Modes of religious experience are shaped by cultural patterns, and when social change shakes and jars the patterns, conventional ways of experiencing the holy disappear too. When an individuated urban culture replaces the thickly clotted symbol system of a preurban society, modalities of religious experience shift. If this happens over a long period of time, religious systems often develop apace. When social change happens swiftly, the cultural symbols may lag behind. But eventually the people experiences the death of its gods. Hence the experience of the "death of God" correlates with a rapid dissolution of traditional cultural patterns and is a frequent characteristic of societies in abrupt transition.

The death-of-god syndrome, whether experienced as a collapse of the symbol system or as an evaporation of the experience of the sacred, can only occur where the controlling symbols of the culture had been more or less uncritically fused with the transcendent god. When a civilization collapses and its gods topple, theological speculation sometimes moves either toward a God whose life center lies outside of culture (Augustine, Barth) or to a thoroughgoing skepticism which can take the form of the "death of God." In our own period, marked by man's historical consciousness' reaching out and encompassing everything in sight, the previous nooks and crannies reserved for the transcendent have all been made immanent. As we shall argue later, only a god of the "not-yet" still transcends history while touching it, the traditional marks of the biblical God, He who though "beyond history" still influences it. Pluralism and radical historicism have become our permanent companions. We know that all doctrines, ideals, institutions and formulations—whether religious or secular—arise within history and must be understood in terms of their historical milieu. How then do we speak of a God who is "in but not of" secular history, who is somehow present in history yet not exhausted in His total being by the historical horizon? How, in short, do we maintain an affirmation of transcendence in a culture whose mood is radical and relentlessly immanentist?

Both Harmon Holcomb and Claude Welch remind me that the efforts of my final chapter to solve this dilemma leave many questions unanswered. Welch correctly insists that we should not confuse doxology with theology, speaking *to* God with speaking *about* Him. Holcomb skillfully uncovers the fact that I have sneaked back to a relatively orthodox position in the end, a position which, however uneasily, Holcomb himself seems to share with me. Both Holcomb and Welch insist that talk to and about God (what some call "religious language") cannot be artificially segregated from talk about other things.

But neither Welch nor Holcomb is able to indicate a way to proceed. Welch's welcome emphasis on the need to encounter God in all of life and not just in a religious or cultic precinct fails nonetheless to say how we talk about anything that really transcends "history," *i.e.*, that which supplies the experiential reference for what we usually talk about. Holcomb ends with an acknowledgment of the "massive unbelief" of the secular world, which he thinks I do not take seriously enough, and the vast chasm separating faith and knowledge.

Both these critics see that I want to move away from any metaphysical dualism, that I want to edge toward a secular theology, a mode of thinking whose horizon is human history and whose idiom is the "political" in the fullest Aristotelian sense of the word. Both suspect that I have not really moved very far. In response, I can only concede that the road ahead does seem treacherous and sometimes almost impassable. I refuse, for the moment, to settle for some brand of simple "religious atheism." That seems too easy somehow. But at the same time I find the available "theistic" options equally unattractive. I have no answer. I can only indicate how I am grappling with this conundrum and where I now hope some new hint of an opening can be found. I am now pursuing the hints, perhaps misleading, of two vagabonds on the periphery of theology, Pierre Teilhard de Chardin and Ernst Bloch. Both men are to some extent pariahs. Chardin was a Jesuit paleontologist whose speculations on the place of man in the cosmos have elicited stern warnings from the Holy See. Ernst Bloch is the eighty-year-old Marxist Revisionist whose irrepressible originality ended in his departure from Communist East Germany. Both of these men represent the outskirts, or the frontiers, of theology. Neither belongs to the club. But if our present crisis teaches us anything, it is that the club is probably finished unless it begins to listen to the outsiders.

For all its wooliness and lack of scientific precision, the thought of Pierre Teilhard de Chardin, with its passion for assigning man a significant place in the vastness of the cosmos and its dynamically immanentist doctrine of God, attracts me. I am not really impressed by those earnest souls who point out the gaps in Teilhard's scientific accuracy, but because I do not think Teilhard's case necessarily rests on the empirical accuracy of his paleontological data. His scientific research really provides Teilhard with little more than a platform from which to launch his singularly biblical vision of man's place in the cosmos. Teilhard's theology is essentially poetic and only accidentally scientific, in the narrow sense. It is really a Christian cosmology, the first we have had for some time that has really engaged the imagination of modern man.

"Since Galileo," writes Teilhard in the newest translation of his works, *The Appearance of Man* (New York: Harper and Row, 1966), "in the eyes of science man has continually lost, one after another, the privileges that made him consider himself unique in the world. Astronomically . . . biologically . . . psychologically . . . Now paradoxically, this same man is in the process re-emerging from his return to the crucible, more than ever *at the head of nature*; since by his very melting back into the general current of convergent cosmogenesis, he is acquiring in our eyes the possibility and power of forming in the heart of space and time, *a single point of humanization for the very stuff of the world.*"

What Teilhard has understood with superb clarity is that the question of God comes to us today "in, with and under" the question of man. The two are inextricable, as we might have imagined had we taken the significance of Jesus seriously. It is for this reason that the contemporary theological rediscovery of the parturient if puzzling thought of Ernst Bloch interests me too, perhaps even more than the work of Teilhard.*

Though there are many differences, both Teilhard and Bloch discuss transcendence in terms of the pressure exerted by the future on the present. They both see that his future is the key to man's being, and they recognize that an authentically open future is only possible where there is a *creature* who can orient himself toward the future and relate himself to reality in terms of this orientation—in short, *a creature who can hope.*

Both Teilhard the maverick Catholic and Bloch the renegade Marxist saw reality as a radically open-ended process. Teilhard detected in the logic of evolution an ever deepening humanization of man and hominization of the universe. Bloch concerned himself with "Man-as-Promise" and mapped out what he called "the ontology of the not yet." Teilhard

---

* Jurgen Moltmann's stunning book *Theologie der Hoffnung* obviously owes a great deal to Bloch as does Wolf-Dieter Marsch's *Gegenwart Christi in der Gesellschaft*. Marsch also has a new small book in the *Stunden buch* series entitled *Hoffen worauf?* It is subtitled *Auseinandersetzung mit Ernst Bloch*.

roamed through the aeons of geological time and the breath-takingly massive universe and focused on the appearance within them of the phenomenon of man, that point where the cosmos begins to think and to steer itself. Bloch's stage for philosophizing is human history, exhumed from its imprisonment in timelessness and launched on a journey into the future. The hope which makes this future possible, Bloch contends, was introduced into the world by the biblical faith. Both Bloch and Teilhard saw what the Germans now call the *"Impuls der Erwartung."* One examined the way cosmic space and time seem to dwarf man, the other the way history seems to buffet him. But then both moved on to emphasize man's growing capacity to apply science and critical reflection in the shaping of his own destiny. Both saw the future not just as that for which man is responsible, but as that for which he now *knows* he is responsible.

My present inclination in response to the provocation of the "death-of-God" theology and the urgent need for a no-nonsense "leveling" in theological discourse is to think that if we can affirm anything which both defines and transcends history it will be the *future* as it lives in man's imagination, nurtured by his memory and actualized by his responsibility. Though space precludes it here, one could explore with great profit the implications this would have for the traditional Christian ideas of eschatology and incarnation. Some of our younger theologians have already begun to do this. Obviously influenced by Teilhard, Karl Rahner once wrote the following moving lines about the Christian man:

> He is a pilgrim on the earth, advancing into the uncertain and going out to venture in brotherly union with all those who plan the future of the world, and he may quite legitimately feel proud of being that creature who plans himself and of being the place (called "spirit" and "freedom") where the great world-machine not only runs its course in exalted clarity but also begins to steer itself (*The Christian and the World*, Rahner, *op. cit.*, p. 213).

Man, seen as the steersman of the cosmos, is the only starting point we have for a viable doctrine of God. Though I think Teilhard may help us in working out this new direction, it is

to Bloch that I wish to devote the rest of the limited space I
have available here, first because most of us know so much
less about Bloch (his work is entirely in German), and second because in the long run I believe he may be even more
influential as theology enters the phase following the "death
of God."

I believe that Bloch's massive *Prinzip Hoffnung,* first published in 1954, a difficult, often unclear but epochal book,
supplies the only serious alternative to Martin Heidegger's
even more opaque *Sein und Zeit* (1927) as a philosophical
partner for theology. Heidegger's interest leads him to the
closed borders and built-in limitations of human existence.
He senses life to be hemmed in and radically finite, but he
still fiercely presses the desperate question of the *"Sein des
Seienden,"* the meaning of the being of that which is. Heidegger's influence on modern theology has been enormous. It is
an influence which I believe, however (as I argued in *The
Secular City* and still hold today), to be almost wholly delete-
rious. Bloch presses the same difficult questions Heidegger
raises but does so within an ontology that seeks to question
and subvert the tight finitude of Heidegger's constricted
human world. Thus while Heidegger plumbs the caliginous
depths of "anxiety," "care" and *"Sein zum Tode,"* if often in
an instructive and revealing way, Bloch deals with that "in-
fatuation with the possible" without which human existence
is unthinkable. "The basic theme of philosophy," argues
Bloch, "is that which is still not culminated, the still unpos-
sessed homeland," and instead of anxiety and death, "philosophy's basic categories should be 'frontier,' 'future,' 'the New'
and the *'Traum nach vorwarts.'* "

Bloch's language is exceedingly difficult to grasp (as is
Heidegger's). His style is sometimes bewildering, sometimes
brilliant. But through it all he keeps insisting that philosophy
should bring these elemental and hope-filled structures of
human existence under critical reflection. Bloch's starting
point in philosophy is the man whose "nature" it is always
and ceaselessly to develop himself and his world. The world is
seen as the correlating field of this humanization.

Bloch considers himself an atheist, as does Heidegger. But
just as many theologians, such as Bultmann and Ott, have

found significant clues for a doctrine of God in Heidegger, there are even more suggestive hints in Bloch. Bloch postulates, for example, a *correspondence* between *man* (as that being who hopes, dreams and is open to history) and the *developing world* itself. He sees this *Entsprechung* (correspondence) between "the subjective content of hope" and the "objectively possible," and tries, often unsuccessfully, to describe it. It is a correspondence, he says, between "subjective" and "objective" hope, and it raises the question in Bloch's mind of an "identity" between man-who-hopes and a structure of reality which supports and nourishes such hope.

At this point the Christian naturally thinks of qualities sometimes attributed to God in theology. Bloch is in no sense unaware of the similarity. He holds that this identity between subjective spontaneity and historical possibility is the "demythologized content of that which Christians have revered as God." So he insists that atheism is the only acceptable stance today in view of the fact that the Christian God has been imprisoned in the stabile categories of a static ontology.

What can a theologian today say about Bloch's tantalizing ideas? Wolf-Dieter Marsch's comment on this point is interesting. Speaking of the identity between subjective hope and sustaining structure in Bloch, he says:

> We can see how close *"Prinzip Hoffnung"* and Christian hope are to each other, and at the same time we can see how far apart they are. This intended "identity" does not like God stand over and against man and his world, but is already contained in the subject-object process and needs only to be developed out of it. Biblically speaking: there is no longer any judgment over the hoping behavior of man, no miracle of grace in the hope that comes ever anew. The nearness of Bloch to Christian hope, however, comes to expression in that man and world, subject and object, are seen in this relationship of correspondence: to the "new man" there corresponds a "new world"—"Behold I make *all* things new" (Revelation 21:5). (*Hoffen worauf*, p. 73.)

There are many further questions one would have to ask about Bloch's work. He does not supply us with a simple way out of the death-of-God morass. I would want to ask, for example, why he *insists* that all possibility is now already incipiently present in what *is*, thus betraying his Aristotelian teleological bias? Why *must* he see hope and the structural grounding of hope as an "identity," revealing now a nineteenth-century German idealist bias? Is it more than his philosophical assumptions which prevent Bloch from affirming a source of hope which is not just part of the given but comes to it from outside? Do these same philosophical assumptions prevent him from being radical enough in his hope? There are times when Bloch's historicism and immanentism (seeing this present material world as all) seem to be in conflict with an authentically *open* world view in which at least the possibility of something entirely other is conceded.

I would also want to suggest that Bloch's message does not take into sufficient account the fate of the individual who always asks what a temporally future fulfillment means for him today. This is the problem which dogs all forms of strictly utopian eschatology. Unrequited hope produces corrosive cynicism unless the future is experienced as present now in a significant way. We need not just the idea of future hope but also something very much like the Johannine idea of "eternity," the present presence of the future, if such cynicism is to be avoided. Jesus' insistence that the New Time is *both* here *and* coming dramatizes this tension.

But Bloch's main theses cannot be easily dismissed, at least from my perspective. Along with Teilhard, he offers the only exit from the theological dead end signaled by the death-of-God theologians. Thus I agree with Wolf-Dieter Marsch when he gingerly suggests that so long as Christians cling to the static *is* as the normative predicate for God, such thinkers as Bloch must rightly continue to regard themselves as atheists. But if theology can leave behind the God who *is* and begin its work with the God who *will be*, or, in biblical parlance, *"He who cometh,"* an exciting new epoch in theology could begin, one in which Ernst Bloch's work would be extraordinarily important. If the present wake is for the God who "is" (and now "was"), this may clear the decks for the God who *will be*. I cannot say for sure that this path will lead anywhere, but it would require a thorough reworking of our major theological categories. We would see Jesus, for example, not as a visitor on earth from some supraterrestrial heaven, but as the one in whom precisely this two-story dualism is abolished for good and who becomes the pioneer and first sign of the coming New Age. We would see the community of faith as those *on the way* to this promised reality, "forgetting what is behind and reaching out for that which lies ahead" (Phil. 3:14). The doctrine of God would become theology's answer to the irrefutable fact that the only way history can be kept open is by "anchoring" that openness somewhere outside history itself, in this case not "above," but ahead.

Still, I would be the worst of imposters if I pretended that in the God of Hope we can immediately affirm the one who will appear when the corpse of the dead God of metaphysical theism is finally interred. He may not appear even after we have buried the God of theism. The whole attempt to work out a new and viable doctrine of God for our time may be fated to fail from the beginning. But I am not yet ready to throw in the towel. Before any of us do, I hope we will exercise the terrible freedom made possible to us by the present *Götterdammerung* of the divinities of Christendom to think as candidly and rigorously as possible about where we go from here.

This then is where I now find myself on those fiendishly difficult questions raised by my final chapter. I still believe that the problem of speaking in a secular fashion of God has important sociological and political aspects. But I believe it has theological dimensions far more baffling than those indicated in *The Secular City*. Though my critics have not given me much help in solving this problem, they have dislodged me from the ground on which I was once stood, and for that I am grateful. They have pushed me along the most promising path I could find. They have turned my face toward the future, where if man meets God again, that encounter must take place.

# Beyond Bonhoeffer?

# The Future of Religionless Christianity

*Harvey Cox*

Recently I was invited to spend several hours with a group of twelve visiting German theologians. They all seemed stunned and disoriented after three weeks in America, bewildered by the confusion of our theological scene. As the meeting started, one of them pleaded with me in a puzzled voice to provide them with a "map of the Protestant theological terrain in America." I told them at once that the situation here was hard to delineate in terms they would understand. I explained that, unlike Germany, we have no relatively homogenous theological community in which movements can be charted and located, where the new school criticizes but builds on the old, where nearly everyone is at least in touch with identifiable mainline currents.

In comparison with Germany, the situation here, I conceded, was chaos. Nevertheless, in response to their insistent urgings, I finally ventured to describe four lines of thought which I took to be significant in American theology today.

First, I mentioned the growing tendency of Catholics and Protestants to read each others' books and journals—not just out of curiosity but to be helped by them. I spoke of the vague beginnings of some ecumenical consensus in theology, well developed in the biblical field, so-so in the field of ethics, still nearly nonexistent in dogmatics. Then I talked about those theologians such as Paul Lehmann who insist that the traditional boundary between ethics and theology must be dissolved, that theology must assume an ethical idiom utilizing the tradition to illuminate our multiple crises in race, economics and world revolution. In the third place, I described those theologians led by Gibson Winter and Colin Williams who see the main theological task today in the reconstruction of the shape (*morphe*) of the church, who use theology to criticize the inherited structures of church life and who wish to re-form the church, as they are apt to say, "around the needs of the world."

Finally, I touched on a group of younger theologians whom Langdon Gilkey and William Hamilton call the death-of-God theologians, those who, beginning either with linguistic analysis or with some variety of existentialist thought, declare that both the word "God" and the whole concept of transcendence have become empty to modern man, and that we must now retranslate the whole business into a strictly secular frame of reference.

I paused after describing these four fairly amorphous tendencies. One of the German theologians, a Berliner, looked up thoughtfully and said, "But Bonhoeffer was interested in these same things and he's been dead for twenty years."

Suddenly I realized he was right. Dietrich Bonhoeffer, the martyr-theologian of the German Resistance—despite the fact that he has become an enigma, a fad, a saint and in some cases an embarrassment in the two decades since his execution by the SS—had his finger on the very issues which continue to torment us. We must be careful not to tear Bonhoeffer out of his context and apply his somewhat fragmentary insights in a wholly different setting. All the same, we cannot yet "move beyond" him because we have not yet faced his challenge seriously. His uncanny capacity to uncover the hidden skeletons in the closets of theology and to see issues coming around the corner means that we have not shaken him. It may be embarrassing to assign readings from someone who has already been written up in a photo essay by *Life*, but as one American theologian put it, "We have to continue studying Bonhoeffer even though he is a fad."

The recent publication in English of extended excerpts from Bonhoeffer's early writings, under the title *No Rusty Swords*, gives us a new opportunity to assess where we now stand on the issues Bonhoeffer raised and how his astonishing theological intelligence might still help us.

Before returning to the four clusters of theological issues I mentioned to the visitors from Germany, it would be well to remind ourselves again that Bonhoeffer was very German and that his insights require considerable transliteration before they make such sense in North America. Not only was he a German, he was also an aristocrat, and as the early letters published in *No Rusty Swords* indicate, his theological credentials were impeccable: Berlin under Harnack, Tübingen under Schlatter, a lecturer in theology in Berlin at the astonishing age of twenty-four. His papers reflect a gifted man deeply in touch with the crises of his age, sensitive to the need for self-respect in Germany, terribly suspicious of the way the Nazis had tied national rebirth to neopaganism.

His year at Union Seminary in New York as a Sloane Fellow in 1930–31 is revealed through letters and notes which give us a glimpse of the strikingly different climate of an American theological institution then. Obviously disturbed, Bonhoeffer wrote in his report: "A seminary in which it can come about that a large number of students laugh out loud in a public lecture at the quoting of a passage from Luther's *De servo arbitrio* on sin and forgiveness because it seems to them to be comic has evidently completely forgotten what Christian theology by its very nature stands for." I doubt if these students, after thirty-five years of rediscovering Reformation theology, would laugh now. But the fact that American and Continental theologians labor in very divergent vineyards is just as true today.

Bonhoeffer's vaunted radicalism grew out of a tradition which was so much a part of him he rarely felt the need to affirm it. His genius was that he could deal with frontier issues, but was able to do so in the light of a theological heritage which he loved and cherished. This is why our American theological enterprise, which often tends to be ahistorical as well as anarchic, can still learn much from him. Too often our traditionalists have no interest in emerging issues and our pioneers feel they must exude a lusty disrespect for anything that happened before 1961. This is why so many new movements in theology end up in old blind alleys.

Bonhoeffer knew the revolutionary power of a tradition understood and applied.

Now let me turn to the four tendencies in current American theology that I mentioned to the German guests, tendencies that prove to me at least that we are still very far from being "beyond Bonhoeffer."

1) Bonhoeffer's interest in the ecumenical promise was early and intense. His papers show him as a determined international conferencegoer, a man who insisted on the unity and catholicity of the church just as the pro-Nazis within the German church were talking about a "German Christianity" and a "national church." He was afraid, he wrote in 1932, that the "polemical necessities of the time of the Reformation" had tended to "isolate German Protestantism in a dangerous way." He energetically rejected the arbitrary dropping of the word "catholic" and substituting the word "Christian" or "universal" in the recitation of the Apostles' Creed as this was practiced by some ultra-Lutherans.

But Bonhoeffer's ecumenical dedication was not just liturgical or organizational. He believed that the various branches of Christendom needed each other as a theological necessity. This conviction was strengthened by serving German-speaking congregations in Spain and Italy and by his year of study in America. Admittedly, Bonhoeffer's ecumenical interest was mainly inter-Protestant, but little else was available at the time. There is no doubt whatever that if he were alive today, he would still be urging the broadest possible basis for the church's theology and pressing for enlargements of the ecumenical perimeter.

2) In his insight into the political relevance of theology, Bonhoeffer was especially contemporary. It took a disturbingly long time for most of the men who later led the anti-Nazi Confessing Church to recognize the horrendous dangers Hitler represented. Niemöller, for example, supported the new "German age" for a year before he began that opposition which finally landed him in Sachsenhausen and Dachau for eight years. Not so Bonhoeffer. Hitler became Chancellor on January 30, 1933. On February 1, Bonhoeffer was cut off the

radio in the midst of a broadcast in which he was criticizing the "leadership principle."

Bonhoeffer's attack on the Nazis was not, like the utterances of some other church leaders, circuitous or indirect. He came to the specific point immediately. Later, as he developed his ethics, he repeatedly emphasized that the church must make its preaching specific and concrete. It must be against *this* war or for *that* economic program and say so with no ambiguity. Is this because the church is infallible in these matters, has some unimpeded line from on high? Not at all. In fact, for Bonhoeffer, the reason was quite the contrary. The church can and must be specific in its ethical and political teaching because it *is* human. It will make mistakes and it can and must repent. As the church of Peter, he insists, it not only confesses Christ; sometimes it betrays him and always it is restored and forgiven. A church which plays it safe by phrasing its ethics in general exhortations, Bonhoeffer says, is untrue to the Gospel. It does not want to be a church under grace. It is also untrue to the teachings of Jesus, which came in highly specific terms and which a faithful church must constantly translate into the equally specific terms of its age. It should never allow its fear of sometimes being wrong to deter it from always being concrete. A church under grace can afford to be concrete since God does not call it to be infallible. He does call it, however, to be faithful and relevant.

Bonhoeffer's ethical thinking has sometimes been used to defend a totally contextualist ethic which Bonhoeffer himself would probably have found dubious. He had nothing against the development and use of principles. He only opposed that cautious form of ethical teaching, all too common in our churches, by which church leaders enunciate principles so general they cut into no one's conscience. He wanted theologians and pastors to take the fearful risk of speaking to actual ethical situations in specific terms lest the historicity and fleshliness of the Gospel evaporate into vapid moralizing.

3) A third area of contemporary theological unrest in America, also one in which Bonhoeffer had considerable interest, is that of the need for a new shape, or *morphe*, for the

church in an urban-industrial society. Bonhoeffer wrote his doctoral dissertation, *Sanctorum Communio,* on the doctrine of the church. In it he refused to identify "church" with any one particular institutional structure. Without falling into the gaseous spiritualism of some kind of "invisible church," he contended that the church exists where man is restored to human community by God's grace. In his early writings he made a good deal out of the fact that Peter's confession, the founding of the church, took place not in or around the temple, but at Caesarea Philippi, that is, on the border of apostasy and paganism. The church always comes into existence, Bonhoeffer believed, where Christ is confessed on the borders of unbelief, doubt and heresy. The church is not at its purest and best in the inner keep of its own spirituality. Its very essence is its engagement with the world.

But Bonhoeffer was no anti-institutional romanticist. He believed that the church lives only in solidarity with the world. But he insisted that the church must have structures which enable it to live this way. Those structures which turn the church in on itself, which make it a rare game sanctuary for premoderns, which prevent it from making a powerful political witness against evil in society—all such structures should be changed. They should be changed not by discarding them and exhorting all Christians to live faithfully as individuals, but by forging every structure of the church in the crucible of service and witness. Bonhoeffer learned the lesson of theologically sound structures the hard way: he saw the German church fail. He heard eloquent pronouncements from synod and pulpit, but saw the church fail to order its life in a way that would stem the tide of fascism.

Bonhoeffer saw the church as one of the empirical institutions contributing to the climate of a country and a world. He was not above participating in the often bruising battle to control it. Today we still need to see that a church can falsify pronouncement by performance, as the American churches have done so long in so many issues. But we must also see, as he did, that the answer to a badly organized and directed church is never no church at all. It is a church constantly renewed and reformed for mission.

4) Surely the most difficult part of Bonhoeffer's work for most people to grasp is his talk about a "nonreligious" interpretation of the Gospel, his suggestion that for the "man come of age" we must find a way to speak of God "in a secular fashion." To some readers this still sounds like sheer nonsense. Religionless Christianity seems to be a *contradictio in adjecto*. But this is just where Bonhoeffer makes his most incisive contribution. If he is misunderstood here, then all he says about the style of church life, about political obedience and about ethics will be lost.

Why do we need a nonreligious interpretation of the Gospel? We have seen that Bonhoeffer believed that the church comes into existence at the edge of paganism. It is shaped both by the thrust of the Gospel and by the changing cultural topography of the world. This is just why we need a nonreligious interpretation. It is necessitated, Bonhoeffer believed, both by the requirements of the Gospel and by the needs of the twentieth-century world.

The Gospel, Bonhoeffer insisted, is the good news of grace. It calls for no moral or intellectual preconditions on the part of the bearer. Nor does it demand any religious precondition. Bonhoeffer used the early Christian debate on circumcision to make this point. The apostles decided quite early that they could not require circumcision of new Christians and still be true to the free grace of God. Likewise today, Bonhoeffer argued, no precondition must be exacted as the price of grace. "Being religious" is the modern equivalent of being circumcised. It must not be made into a precondition of grace, since God's grace has already been lavished on man and is free. Also, as a student of Karl Barth, Bonhoeffer had learned that religion is not always a good thing, that it can become man's way to escape God as easily as it becomes man's way to serve Him. In short, his first reason for de-religionizing the Gospel was strictly theological.

But Bonhoeffer also argued for a religionless Christianity because of the ethos of the modern world. He saw in the process of secularization, which he dated from about the time of the Renaissance, not some seasonal tempest which would soon blow over, but a coming to fruition of much that Christianity had planted in the soil of Western civilization. In this respect Bonhoeffer stands closer to some Catholic humanists, to the traditional Catholic admiration for *urbanitas,* than he does to many Protestants. As an astute observer of his fellow men, he thought he detected the appearance in our time of a new type of person later termed by Helmut Gollwitzer as the "areligious personality." Also, unlike so many theologians, Catholic and Protestant, Bonhoeffer affirmed much of the impact of the Enlightenment. He admired and celebrated man's growing power over nature, his aesthetic genius, his capacity to generate values. He pleaded with fellow theologians to begin fashioning theologies which would speak to man not in his weakness, sickness and death, but in his maturity, strength and responsibility. He did not feel that to acclaim man's stature somehow detracted from the glory of God.

To the very end Bonhoeffer lived with joy on the edge of paganism. In his final days he exchanged ideas with a Communist cellmate, the nephew of Molotov. Bonhoeffer loved and admired the atheists and agnostics with whom he lived his last hours. No doubt they deepened his determination to find a nonreligious interpretation of the Gospel. Standing on that difficult border between church and world, he had an unshakable certainty that the God of grace could speak even to the nonreligious man. True both to earth and Heaven, both to God and man, he saw with rare clarity that such a stance would necessitate far-reaching changes in future theology.

In short, Bonhoeffer wanted us to believe in man and his possibilities, and he did not feel that this should weaken our faith in God. This is obviously another point where we would be arrogant to claim that we are "beyond Bonhoeffer." The enormous and somewhat unmerited attention now being lavished on Teilhard de Chardin surely shows that many people today wish to acknowledge man's crucial place in the cosmos while still affirming God's encompassing sovereignty. They turn to Chardin, whose thought is often far less than intellectually precise, mainly because few other theologians have dared to strike out in this direction. Chardin also wanted to celebrate man in his strength.

But need this man be "nonreligious"? Since for Bonhoeffer religion implied an element of dependency, a weakness which must be matched by a strength from elsewhere, a need for answers not to be found by man himself, on his terms, the "man come of age" would *not* be religious. There will be those today, of course, contending with some justification that religion need not mean all these things and that therefore Bonhoeffer's nonreligious interpretation would not be as radical as it first sounds. Perhaps they are right. Perhaps the meaning of the word "religion" can be so radically redefined that Bonhoeffer's challenge will evaporate. But I doubt it. For the vast majority of people today, especially in America, "religion" still means very much what he had in mind.

Bonhoeffer was utterly serious. He emphasized time and time again that God had founded his church "beyond religion," that to be a Christian was "not to be religious in a particular sense, but to be a man." He meant that we should not deplore, but greet the appearance of the areligious personality. He meant that Christians should not be trapped into some crusade to defend "religion" of whatever sort against the threat of "atheism" or of "secularism." After all, certain types of atheism are closer to biblical faith than are certain types of religion. Pompey was shocked when he pushed his way into the inner court of the Jewish Temple after conquering Jerusalem and found no statue. He became convinced that the Jews were really atheists, which as far as his gods were concerned they probably were. The early Christians were maimed and murdered not principally because they believed in Jesus, but because they did *not* believe in Caesar. They were the forerunners, Bonhoeffer would argue, of the areligious personalities of our age.

But how *shall* we speak of God to the secular man? Bonhoeffer gave no answer. Still, from the very issues to which he devoted his life, we may get some hint. Gathering up those interests, we could speculate as follows:

1) A divided church will not speak to the man come of age. Mired in its own provincialisms, obsessed with defenses of its partial truths, it elicits hardly more than a yawn from the people Bonhoeffer wished to address. If reconciliation and

authentic community constitute God's gift to the world, then a dismembered church contravenes its own message. Unity is not something for Christians to enjoy among themselves. It is a prerequisite of mission.

2) A church which eschews politics, or worse still, uses politics to shore up its own position in the world, will never speak to secular man. Ministers and nuns on picket lines for racial justice today are not just signs of the church's "social concern." They are evangelists, telling modern man what the Gospel says. The church which remains securely within the "spiritual realm" will annoy no one and convince no one, for secular man is a political animal *par excellence,* and that indispensable dimension of the Gospel which goes "beyond politics" begins after, not before, the political obedience of Christians.

3) A church whose ethical pronouncements remain generic and abstract will never speak to the secular man. He does not live "in general." He lives his life in a particular place, doing a certain job, faced with specific issues. Vague moral advice does not interest him. Specific ethical demands may infuriate him, stimulate him, or encourage him. But at least he will hear them, which is all the church can ever succeed in accomplishing. Whether he believes or obeys is not, in the final analysis, determined by the church but by the Spirit of God at work within him.

Thus the answer to the fourth issue raised by Bonhoeffer, how to speak of God to the secular man, will only be given to us as we grapple faithfully with the previous three. Of course Bonhoeffer has been misunderstood and misused. He will be again. Of course theological fads are always dangerous. But we are in no sense finished with Bonhoeffer. Nor do I believe we can move "beyond" him until we begin to be the kind of church he knew we must be, a church which lives on the border of unbelief, which speaks with pointed specificity to its age, which shapes its message and mission not for its own comfort but for the health and renewal of the world.

# DATE DUE

| | | | |
|---|---|---|---|
| MY 10 '67 | DEC 2 '74 | | |
| DEC N6 '69 | | | |
| JUN 24 '70 | NOV 2 '75 | | |
| JUN 24 '70 | NOV 16 '75 | | |
| OCT 12 '70 | MAR 9 '78 | | |
| OCT 26 '70 | APR 17 '78 | | |
| | SEP 66 '79 | | |
| FEB 14 '71 | AUG 17 1983 | | |
| | MAR 31 '89 | | |
| MAR 27 '73 | | | |
| NOV 26 '73 | | | |
| AUG 22 '74 | | | |
| NOV 13 '74 | | | |
| GAYLORD | | | PRINTED IN U.S.A. |